# not lame! Makoto's cross-stitch super collection
### very cool!

The information in this book was originally published in the following two titles:
Hop, Stitch, Jump!
Copyright ©2009 Oozu Makoto
My Stitch Book
Copyright ©2008 Oozu Makoto
Both originally published in Japanese language by Byakuya Shobo
English language rights, translation and production by World Book Media, LLC
For international rights inquiries contact: info@worldbookmedia.com

www.fwmedia.com

First Published in the United States of America by North Light Books,

an imprint of F+W Media, Inc., 4700 East Galbraith Road, Cincinnati,

Ohio 45236. (800) 289-0963. First edition.

Printed in China

ISBN-10: 1-4403-0925-6

ISBN-13: 978-1-4403-0925-0

10 9 8 7 6 5 4 3 2 1

# not lame! Makoto's cross-stitch very cool! super collection

**Makoto Oozu**

NORTH
LIGHT
BOOKS

Cincinatti, Ohio

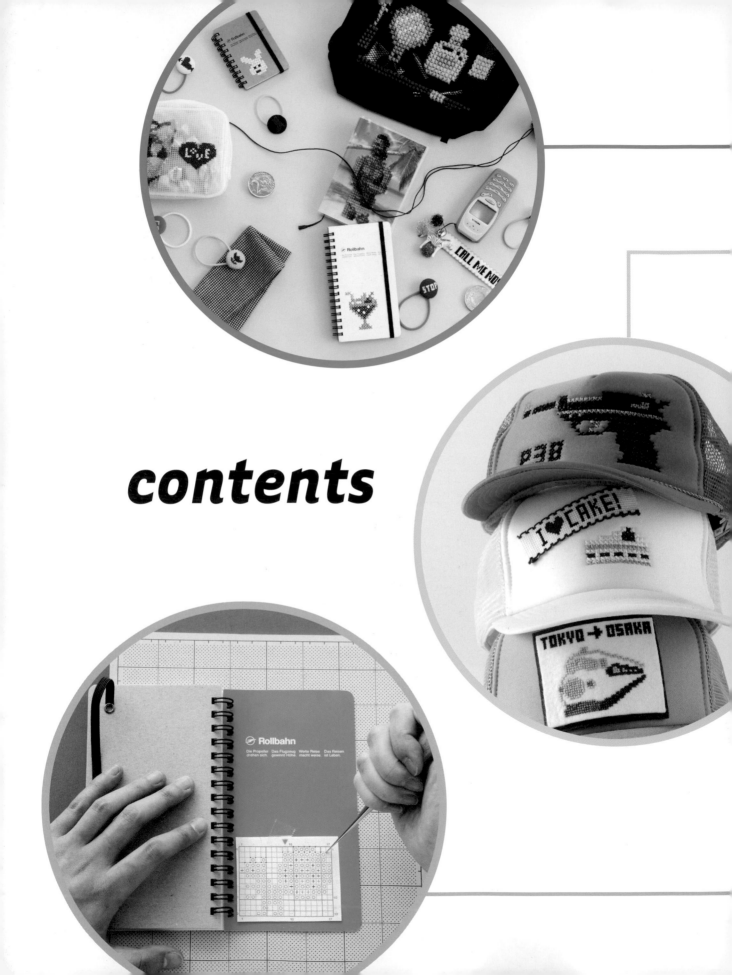

# contents

# Part 1. X-Stitch Motifs

# Part 2. X-Stitching on Gear

# Part 3. How to Make

# Hello!

My name is Makoto Oozu, and I am a cross-stitch designer. Thank you for picking up my book! To tell you the truth, I am really a very clumsy crafter. I have pricked my finger countless times with a sewing needle. Every time I sit down at the sewing machine, the sewing threads get tangled the moment I press the pedal. And just looking at knitting instructions makes my head spin. But I love cross-stitching. Yes, cross-stitching! It is so simple that anyone—even people like me—can enjoy.

Cross-stitch is the craft of embroidering fabric with tiny x-shaped stitches, made into colorful patterns and shapes. All the projects in this book use this basic x-shaped cross-stitch. Keep in mind, these projects are not elaborate work of fiber art to be framed and displayed, untouched for eternity—they are artful, playful, everyday pieces to wear and enjoy.

Some projects experiment with materials, such as yarn, paper, vinyl, even baseball caps, but you're always just using the basic cross-stitch. Here's a trick: You can cross-stitch with anything that can be threaded through a needle...and anything a needle can pierce!

For beginners, I would recommend finding a simple project that makes you happy, and work at it at your own pace, whenever you have the time. This way, you start a good relationship with your needle and thread!

I hope I can share my sheer enjoyment for this craft with all of you, and that this book inspires you to create, too.

Let's get started!

—**Makoto Oozu**

# Part 1
## X-Stitch Motifs

# Robots

These robots are designed to do your bidding, even without batteries. You can cross-stitch these characters on a number of different projects, bringing delight wherever they go!

*Cross-stitch patterns for Robots on page 52*

Dinosaurs may not roam the earth anymore, but they're far from forgotten! Try these on curtains or pillowcases, or in a framed, stitched primordial landscape scene.

*Cross-stitch patterns for Dinosaurs on page 56*

# Monsters and More!

These monsters aren't scary, they're fun! There are many projects for Halloween that could use this spooky company.

*Cross-stitch patterns for Monsters and More on page 60*

# Spaced Out

"That's one small stitch for man..." These spaced-out friends would look great on pajamas or cross-stitched as a border on bedroom curtains.

*Cross-stitch patterns for Spaced Out on page 64*

# Grasshopper and Friends

Leave the bugs alone—or these bugs, at least! They don't fly and they don't bite, but they do look very cute cross-stitched on a variety of projects.

*Cross-stitch patterns for Grasshopper and Friends on page 68*

Bring the underwater world just a little bit closer with these adorable creatures. Cross-stitch these patterns on your bathroom towels or frame them and display them as art.

*Cross-stitch patterns for Sea Creatures on page 72*

# Globe Trotting

Viva embroidery! Say sayonara to fussy stitching! Travel the world without leaving your chair with these charming, world-class designs.

*Cross-stitch patterns for Globe Trotting on page 76*

# Electronic Gear

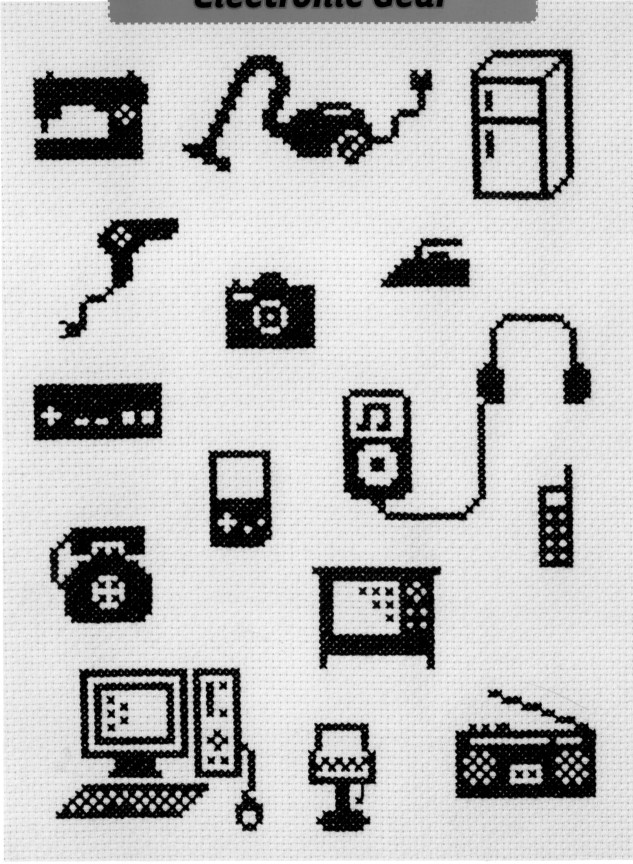

Who thought electronic gear could look so cute? You can cross-stitch these icons on hats, T-shirts, or small accessories to make them sing.

*Cross-stitch patterns for Electronic Gear on page 84*

# Part 2

**X-Stitching on Gear**

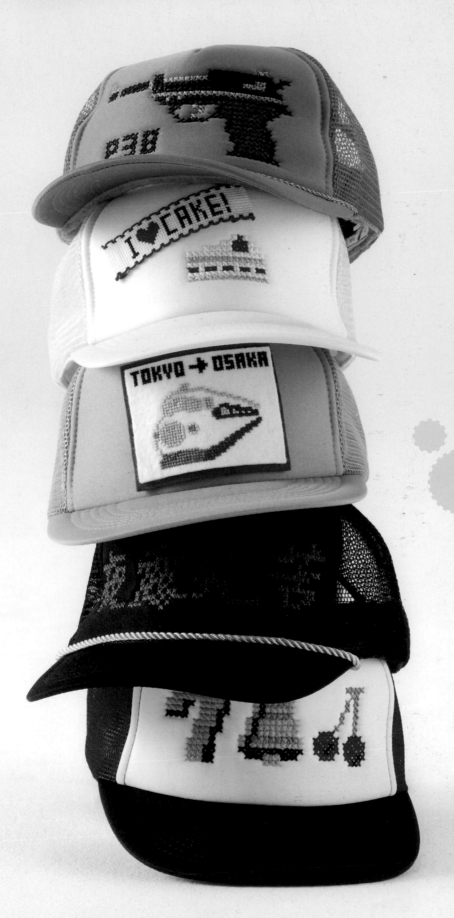

Sew your own motif on a baseball cap and wear it to town! Baseball cap fabric tends to be thick, so make sure you use a thimble when you're stitching these projects.

*Cross-stitch patterns for Hop Stitch Caps on page 88*

# Time Travel Safari Shirt

Feeling nostalgic for the old days? No, I mean really old—think prehistoric.
These dinosaur designs are the essence of "retro".

*Cross-stitch patterns for Time Travel Safari Shirt on page 93*

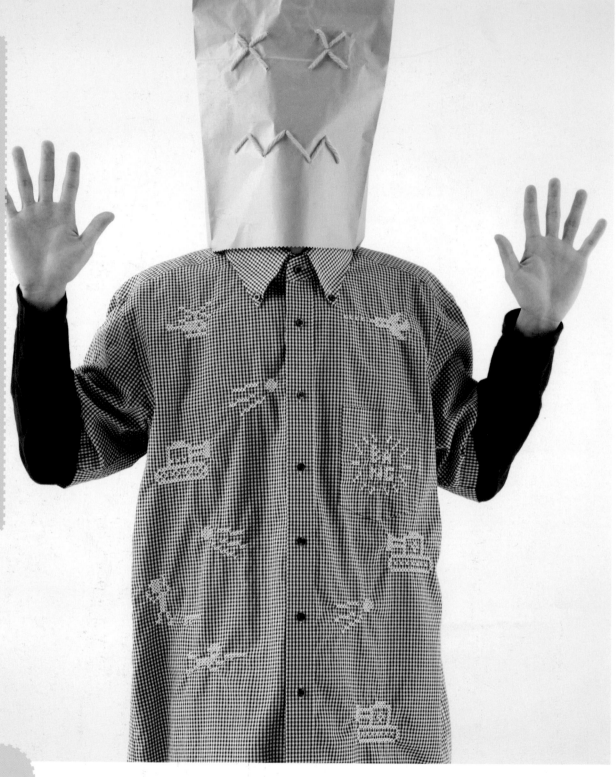

Bang! Pow! Your favorite gingham shirt, invaded by neon 8-bit video game creatures! (Crafty tip: Gingham is perfect fabric for cross-stitch because you can use the checks as your grid!)

*Cross-stitch patterns for 8-Bit Gingham Shirt on page 100*

One, two, three, KNOCKOUT! Underneath it all, you're still a champ.

*Cross-stitch patterns for Short Shorts on page 103*

# Preppy Skull Sweater

Forget an alligator, how about a skull on a sweater? Note that on knit fabric the stitch size for a cross-stitch design will be determined by the stitch size of the knitted fabric. If the knit stitch is too fine, you can also cross-stitch on waste canvas (see page 45).

*Cross-stitch patterns for Preppy Skull Sweater on page 104*

# Eco Bags for XS Lovers

Why not personalize your grocery tote with cross-stitch designs? These also make fun and practical gifts. Use waste canvas (see page 45) when stitching onto regular fabric bags.

*Cross-stitch patterns for Eco Bags for XS Lovers on page 105*

# Beautiful Bug Pillows

While real insects can be creepy, these cross-stitched bugs are the best—especially "crawling" across throw pillows.

*Cross-stitch patterns for Beautiful Bug Pillows on page 112*

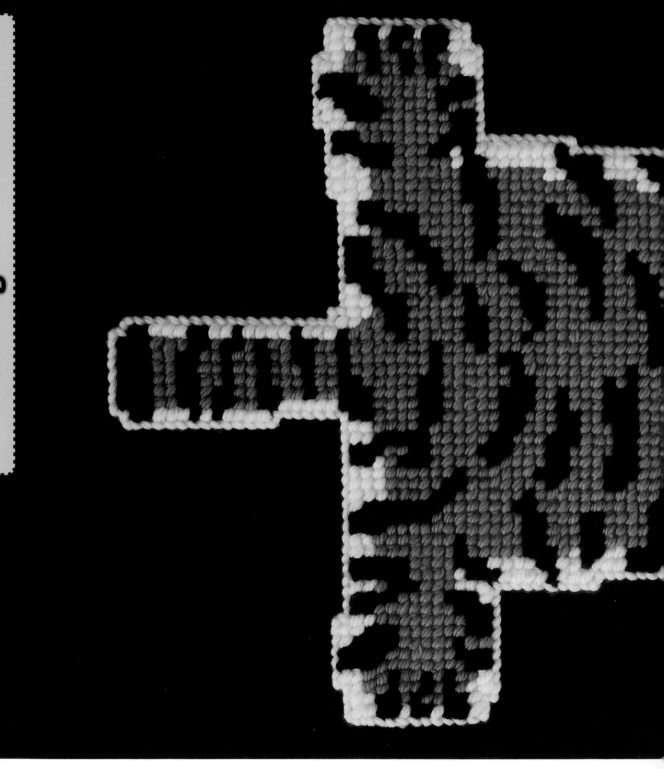

Such a cute little rug should be at the front door of your home or front-and-center in your living room. The full, fluffy texture makes it hard to believe it's all cross-stitch! This project is made with plastic canvas and yarn.

*Cross-stitch patterns for Faux Tiger Doormat on page 116*

# In the Bag

A place for everything and everything in its place. Stitch up some eye candy on small, everyday accessories.

*Cross-stitch patterns for In the Bag on page 118.*

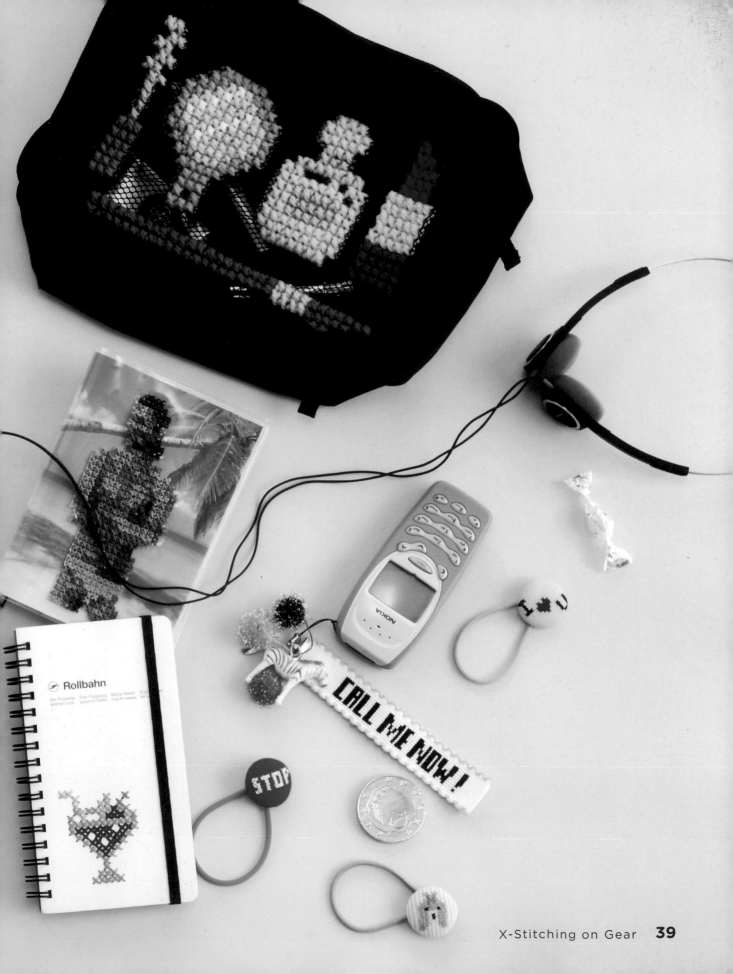

# 3-D Panel

Who said dinosaurs are extinct? This room panel's 3-D effect brings even the most long-gone creatures back to life.

*Cross-stitch patterns for 3-D Panel on page 124*

# Part 3
## How to Make

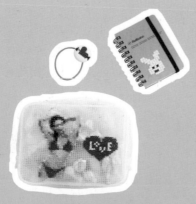

# Cross-Stitch Materials & Tools

## Get to Know Your Tools and Materials

First, gather the basic tools for cross-stitching. You will find most of them at craft or sewing stores. They come in many designs, so find (and use!) your favorites.

**Embroidery floss:** Floss is made up of 6 strands of thread. The floss used in this book is DMC No. 25. For each project, pull out the number of strands called for in the design. The finished design will look different if different numbers of strands are used. Cut floss to about 16" (about 40 cm) long when embroidering as it is more likely to tangle and knot if it's longer. Each thread has a unique color number (for consistency).

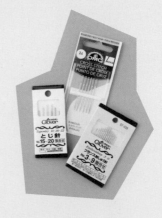

**Needles:** When stitching on cross-stitch fabric, use tapestry needles with a blunt tip. Use pointed-tip French embroidery needles when stitching on finely woven fabric and a heavy duty pointed-tip needle when stitching on thicker fabrics. Use a tapestry needle when embroidering with yarns.

**Scissors:** Use sharp-pointed scissors for snipping embroidery floss ends.

**Embroidery hoop:** Used to hold the fabric taut; especially helpful for stitching on thin and soft fabrics.

**Aida fabric:** For counted cross-stitch, use Aida cross-stitch fabric or linen (with a visible weave). Both have squares that are easy to count. Aida fabric unravels easily, so whipstitch the fabric edges before you begin to stitch your pattern.

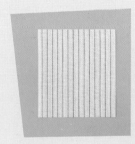

**Waste canvas:** Used for stitching designs on uneven fabrics (like denim or knits). Waste canvas can be basted onto the fabric you want to stitch on, or you can use waste canvas with an adhesive. After you stitch on this canvas, you can remove it, one thread at a time after dampening the waste canvas.

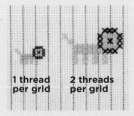

**Stitch band:** Fabric band made especially for cross-stitching. Its edges are finished, so it's perfect for borders, trims, or such things as name tags.

**11-count fabric**     **14-count fabric**

**Count number:** Denotes how many squares are in 1" of fabric. The bigger the number is, the smaller each square is. Note that the finished size of the design will differ when using fabrics with different counts.

**1 thread per grid**     **2 threads per grid**

**Threads per grid:** Each stitch on a pattern is represented by one square "grid". A regular cross-stitch is made by stitching "over 1 thread" (over a single thread) of fabric (Aida or waste canvas, etc.). A pattern can be enlarged by "stitching over 2 threads". This doubles the design size (see photo on left).

# Stitch Guide

## Basic Stitches

Let's take a close look at cross-stitch, one square at a time. If you make a mistake, just bring the needle back slowly through the fabric, undoing the last stitch you made.

One of the perks of cross-stitch: It's easy to start over.

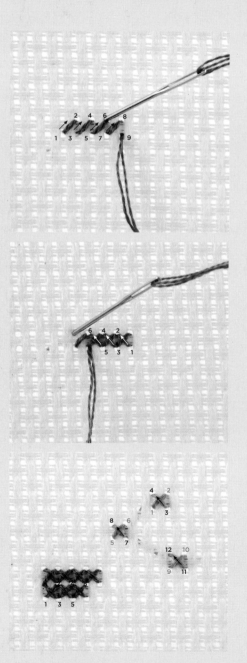

### Basic Cross-Stitch

Following your pattern, one row at a time, pull the needle to the front of the fabric at 1, back at 2, to the front at 3, and back at 4, and so on, creating a row of parallel diagonal stitches (as shown at left). For a smooth finish, tug gently on each stitch so it sits against the fabric without puckering it.

Once you reach the end of the row, stitch back along the row to complete the x-shapes.

When stitching a second row of stitches, follow the same stitch order as in the first row. The cross-threads of each stitch should follow in the same direction.

To make single stitches (not in a row), pull the needle to the front at 9 and back at 6, to the front at 7 and back at 4 (as shown at left). Do not pull the thread too hard.

### How to Start a Row (Method 1)

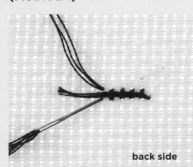

back side

Insert the needle and unknotted thread through the fabric and leave a 1" (25 mm) tail on the back side. As you stitch, wrap the tail with the thread on the back side.

### How to Start a Row (Method 2)

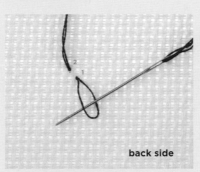

back side

Separate the strands evenly and make a loop. Make a circle knotting the end of the threads. Make a stitch and insert the needle through the loop. Draw it closed.

### How to Finish a Row

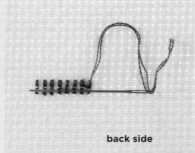

back side

Without making a knot in the thread, insert the needle and pull thread through the loops on the back side. The tail is secured. Snip the end.

### How to Use Waste Canvas

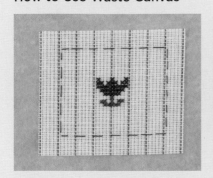

Cut a square of waste canvas that is bigger than the pattern. Baste it to the base fabric using large stitches with any sort of thread. Cross-stitch through the waste canvas, following the pattern.

After finishing stitching, dampen the waste canvas (water in a spray bottle works well). Remove the basting thread and pull out the waste canvas one thread at a time, working from the edges.

Because of the thickness of the waste canvas, the pattern will have a smoother finish if you make your stitches tighter than normal.

## Back Stitch

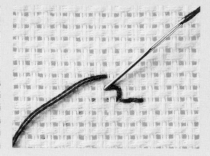

To sew a continuous straight line, use a back stitch. Bring the needle and thread to the front at 1 then insert it through at 2. Bring it to the front again at 3.

Insert the needle and thread through at 1 again. One back stitch. Moving to the left, repeat: 4, 3, 5, 4, 6, 5...and so on.

Use the back stitch for creating zigzag patterns, too.

## Straight Stitch

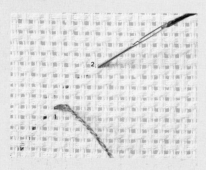

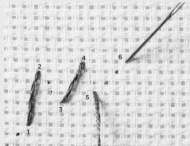

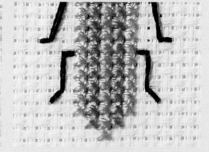

Bring the needle to the front at 1 then insert it through at 2.

Repeat for 3 and 4, 5 and 6, and wherever individual straight stitches are needed. This stitch can be used at any length or in any direction.

Combined with small back stitches, the straight stitch is perfect for insect legs!

## French Knot

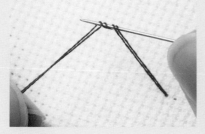  

Bring the the needle and thread all the way through the fabric. Wind the thread around the needle a few times.

Tip the needle toward the fabric, and insert it beneath a very small length of fabric, taking a tiny stitch.

Slowly pull the needle through the fabric, and pull the wrapped thread off the needle, to finish the French knot.

## Other Cross-Stitch Materials

There are several projects in this book that use novel materials and fabrics but still use the basic cross-stitch. You can personalize just about anything with cross-stitching.

### Paper

 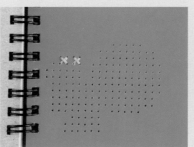

### Felt

For thick paper, you must first pierce holes with an awl. Photocopy the cross-stitch pattern, tape it to the paper you will stitch on, and pierce the pattern and paper with the awl. Place a craft cutting mat (or layers of newspaper) beneath the paper to avoid scratching the table.

Cross-stitch through the holes. Using this technique, you can stitch on leather and vinyl, too. An awl is very sharp—be careful!

Felt is a great craft fabric because its edges do not need finishing. Cut it to the desired shape, and attach a double-sided adhesive sheet (found at craft stores) to make it into a patch.

### Knits

You can cross-stitch right over chunky knit stitches. Use waste canvas on smaller knits, if it is hard to see the rows.

### Gingham Fabric

Use the natural grid of the checkered fabric as a stitch guide. The size and shape of the motif will vary when the checks are rectangular.

### Grid/Lattice Materials

There are a lot of materials that have mesh-like or a lattice pattern that can be used for cross-stitch. Avoid pulling the thread too much when using the fabric, which may wrinkle easily.

**Cross-Stitch with Yarn:** You don't need to cross-stitch with embroidery thread. Broaden the scope and scale of your projects by using yarn. Use a tapestry needle when stitching with yarn.

### Mesh Objects

Cross-stitch on small household items made from mesh, such as this plain pen holder.

### Plastic Canvas or Vinyl Netting

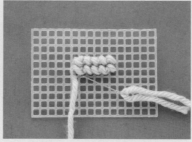

Plastic canvas or vinyl netting can be found at most craft stores. Using thick yarns will give the piece a fluffy texture. Cut the canvas into fun shapes—the edges do not need finishing.

### Pegboard

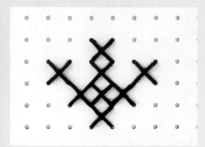

Anything with an even grid of holes can become cross-stitch material...even pegboard. When you start seeing the world in terms of stitching potential, you know you've become obsessed!

# CHARTS

## A Guide to Cross-Stitch Patterns

There are patterns for all projects in this book, and each one lists the color number of the embroidery thread called for in the design as well as the materials and fabrics needed. Once you get used to cross-stitch, you can make original designs from any number of materials.

## How to Read Pattern Charts for Projects in Part 1

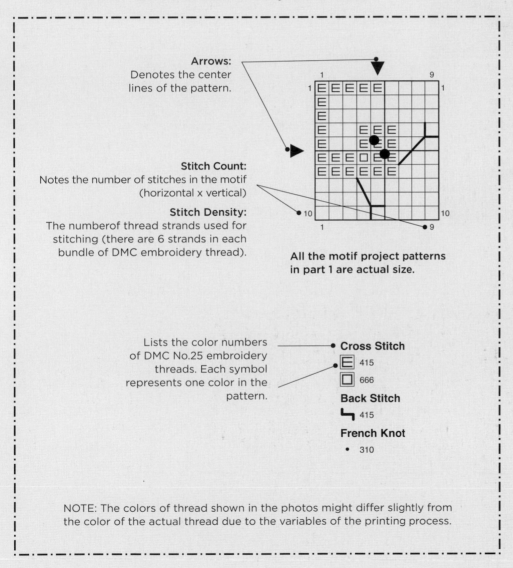

**Arrows:**
Denotes the center lines of the pattern.

**Stitch Count:**
Notes the number of stitches in the motif (horizontal x vertical)

**Stitch Density:**
The numberof thread strands used for stitching (there are 6 strands in each bundle of DMC embroidery thread).

All the motif project patterns in part 1 are actual size.

Lists the color numbers of DMC No.25 embroidery threads. Each symbol represents one color in the pattern.

**Cross Stitch**
E  415
□  666

**Back Stitch**
∟  415

**French Knot**
•  310

NOTE: The colors of thread shown in the photos might differ slightly from the color of the actual thread due to the variables of the printing process.

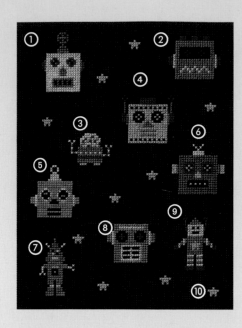

# Robots (from page 10)

**Fabric:** Aida 14 count/ 310 (black)
**Thread:** DMC No. 25 floss
**Stitch Density:** 2 strands

## 1
**Stitch Count:** 19 x 26
**Cross-stitch**

| | |
|---|---|
| + | 415 |
| □ | 3790 |
| − | 666 |
| ✕ | 310 |

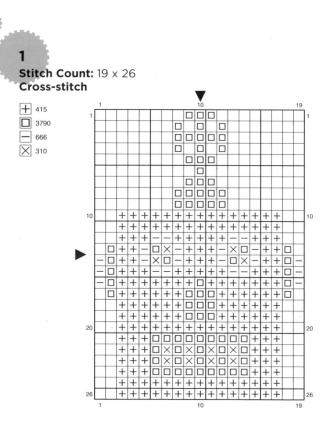

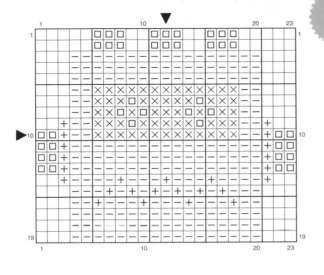

**2**
**Stitch Count:** 23 x 19
**Cross-stitch**

| | |
|---|---|
| + | 415 |
| □ | 666 |
| − | 798 |
| × | 310 |

**3**
**Stitch Count:** 19 x 14
**Cross-stitch**

| | |
|---|---|
| + | 415 |
| □ | 157 |
| − | 972 |
| × | 666 |
| ✳ | 906 |
| ∣ | 3790 |
| # | 798 |

**4**
**Stitch Count:** 23 x 21
**Cross-stitch**

| | |
|---|---|
| □ | 666 |
| − | 3790 |
| × | 972 |
| ✳ | 310 |
| ∣ | 740 |

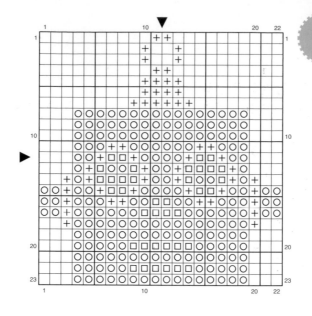

## 5
**Stitch Count:** 22 x 23
**Cross-stitch**

| + | 415 |
| ○ | 906 |
| □ | 310 |

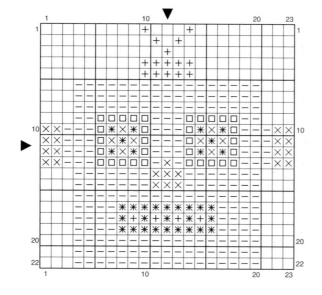

## 6
**Stitch Count:** 23 x 22
**Cross-stitch**

| + | 415 | — | 552 | ✳ | 310 |
| □ | 666 | ✕ | 972 | | |

## 7
**Stitch Count:** 16 x 25
**Cross-stitch**

| + | 415 |
| E | 798 |
| — | 310 |
| I | 972 |
| # | 740 |

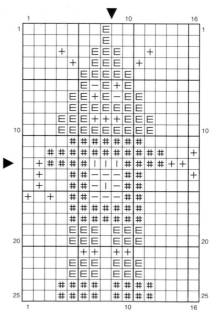

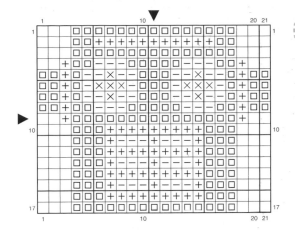

### 8
**Stitch Count:** 21 x 17
**Cross-stitch**

| + | 415 |
| □ | 893 |
| — | 310 |
| ✕ | 666 |

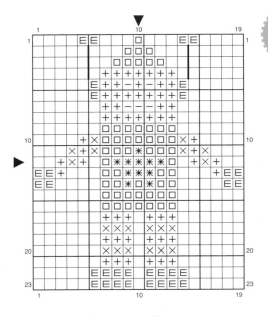

### 9
**Stitch Count:** 19 x 23
**Cross-stitch**

| + | 415 |
| E | 666 |
| □ | 798 |
| — | 310 |
| ✕ | 3790 |
| ✳ | 972 |

**Straight Stitch**

| ⌐ | 3790 |

### 10
**Stitch Count:** 5 x 4
**Cross-stitch**

| □ | 972 |

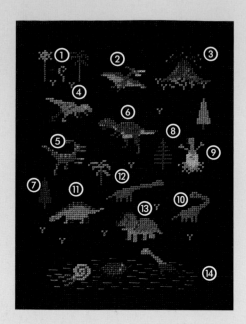

# Dinosaurs (from page 12)

**Fabric:** Aida 14 count/ 310 (black)
**Thread:** DMC No. 25 floss
**Stitch Density:** 2 strands

## 1

**Stitch Count:** 25 x 19
**Cross-stitch**

| E | 702 |
|---|-----|
| □ | 3345 |
| — | 869 |

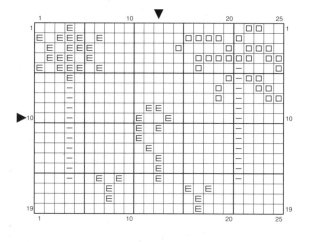

## 2

**Stitch Count:** 23 x 13
**Cross-stitch**

| + | 552 |
|---|-----|
| E | 972 |
| □ | 415 |
| — | 869 |
| X | 740 |
| ✳ | 841 |

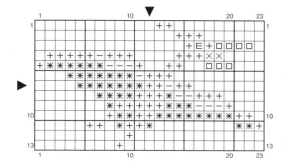

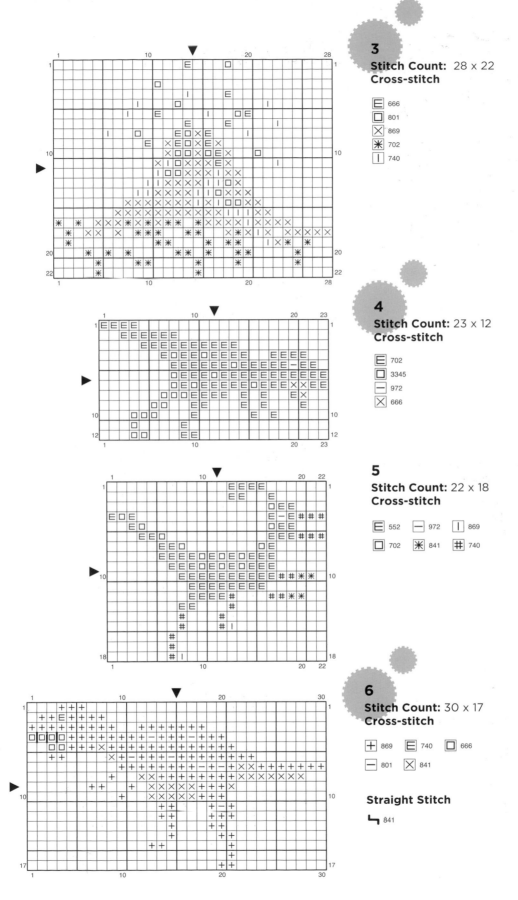

### 3
**Stitch Count:** 28 x 22
**Cross-stitch**

- E 666
- □ 801
- ✕ 869
- ✳ 702
- I 740

### 4
**Stitch Count:** 23 x 12
**Cross-stitch**

- E 702
- □ 3345
- — 972
- ✕ 666

### 5
**Stitch Count:** 22 x 18
**Cross-stitch**

- E 552
- — 972
- I 869
- □ 702
- ✳ 841
- # 740

### 6
**Stitch Count:** 30 x 17
**Cross-stitch**

- + 869
- E 740
- □ 666
- — 801
- ✕ 841

**Straight Stitch**

- ⌐ 841

**7**
**Stitch Count:** 7 x 16
**Cross-stitch**

E 702
□ 869

**8**
**Stitch Count:** 9 x 16
**Cross-stitch**

E 3345
□ 869

**9**
**Stitch Count:** 13 x 18
**Cross-stitch**

E 801  X 415  I 740
□ 702  ✳ 436

**10**
**Stitch Count:** 19 x 15
**Cross-stitch**

E 893
— 801

**11**
**Stitch Count:** 27 x 11
**Cross-stitch**

E 798  X 702  I 740
□ 801  ✳ 436

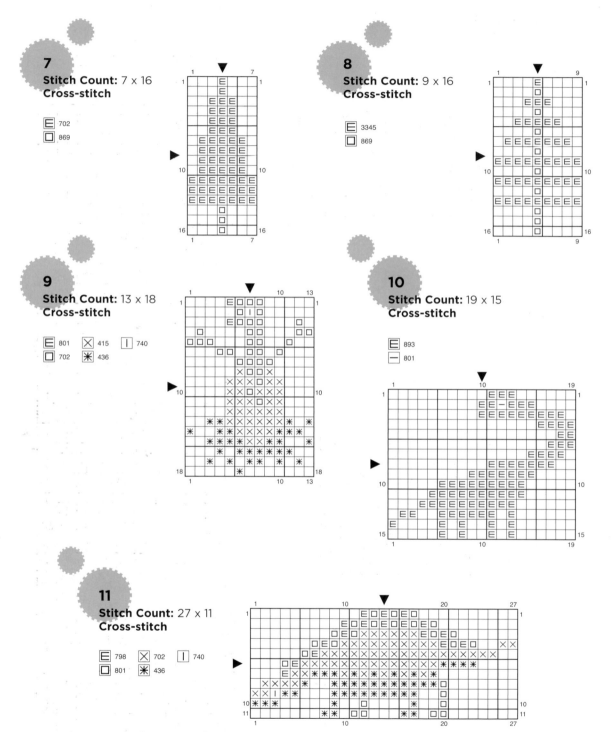

## 12

**Stitch Count:** 29 × 11
**Cross-stitch**

E  798
□  552

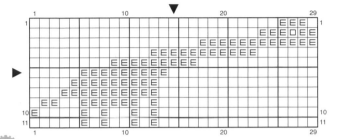

## 13

**Stitch Count:** 24 × 15
**Cross-stitch**

+  801
E  740
□  3345
—  436

## 14

**Stitch Count:** 76 × 20
**Cross-stitch**

E  702
□  415
—  801
X  869
✳  972
|  3345
#  893

**Straight Stitch**  ⌐  801
                      ⌐  798

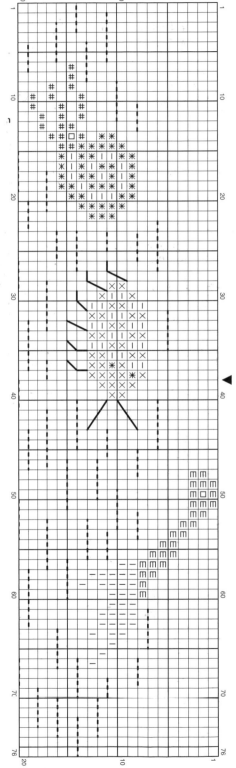

# Monsters and More

**(from page 13)**

**Fabric:** Aida 14 count/ 310 (black)
**Thread:** DMC No. 25 floss
**Stitch Density:** 2 strands

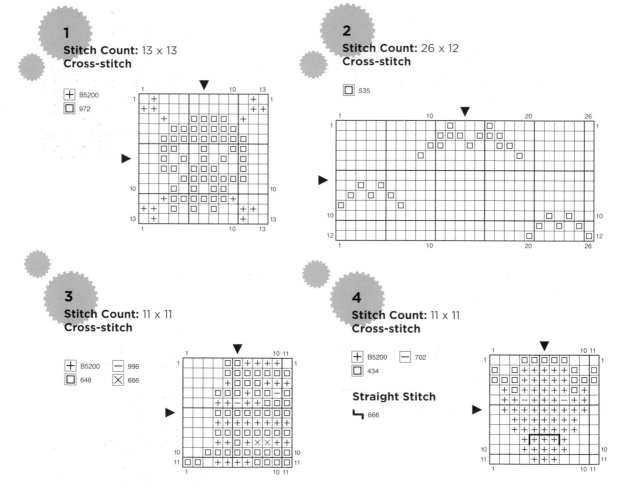

## 1
**Stitch Count:** 13 x 13
**Cross-stitch**

+ B5200
□ 972

## 2
**Stitch Count:** 26 x 12
**Cross-stitch**

□ 535

## 3
**Stitch Count:** 11 x 11
**Cross-stitch**

+ B5200    — 996
□ 648    ☒ 666

## 4
**Stitch Count:** 11 x 11
**Cross-stitch**

+ B5200    — 702
□ 434

**Straight Stitch**

⌐ 666

## 5

**Stitch Count:** 22 x 20
**Cross-stitch**

☐ 972
— 434

**Straight Stitch** ⌐ 434

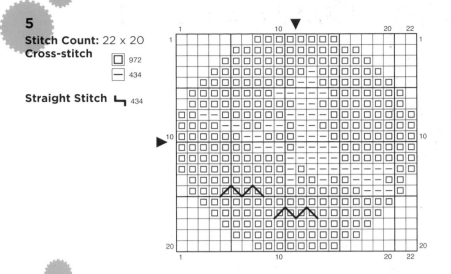

## 6

**Stitch Count:** 15 x 10
**Cross-stitch**

☐ 369
— 972
✕ 666

**Straight Stitch**

⌐ 369

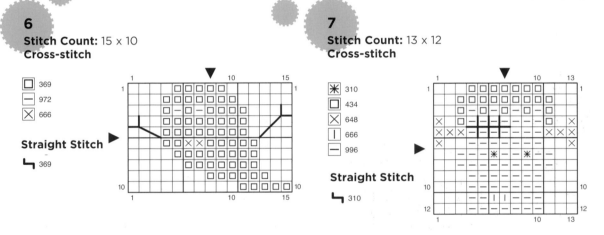

## 7

**Stitch Count:** 13 x 12
**Cross-stitch**

✳ 310
☐ 434
✕ 648
❘ 666
— 996

**Straight Stitch**

⌐ 310

## 8

**Stitch Count:** 14 x 10
**Cross-stitch**

☐ 535
— 972

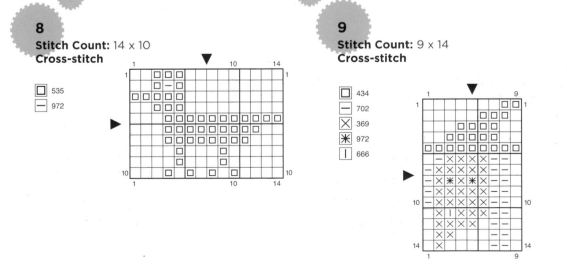

## 9

**Stitch Count:** 9 x 14
**Cross-stitch**

☐ 434
— 702
✕ 369
✳ 972
❘ 666

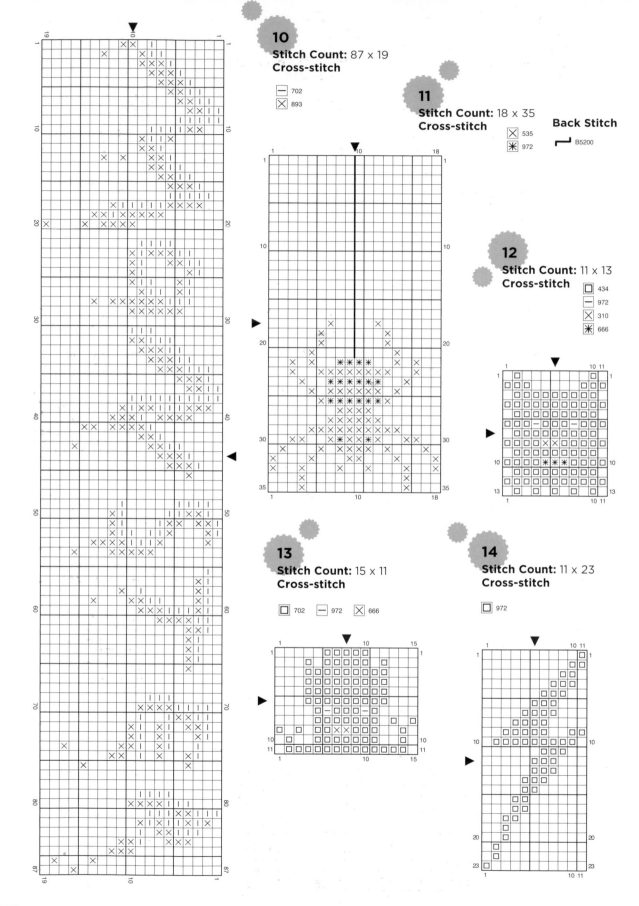

**10**
**Stitch Count:** 87 x 19
**Cross-stitch**

— 702
☒ 893

**11**
**Stitch Count:** 18 x 35
**Cross-stitch**

☒ 535
✳ 972

**Back Stitch**

⌐ B5200

**12**
**Stitch Count:** 11 x 13
**Cross-stitch**

☐ 434
— 972
☒ 310
✳ 666

**13**
**Stitch Count:** 15 x 11
**Cross-stitch**

☐ 702    — 972    ☒ 666

**14**
**Stitch Count:** 11 x 23
**Cross-stitch**

☐ 972

**15**
Stitch Count: 15 x 13
Cross-stitch  ☐ 702  — 740

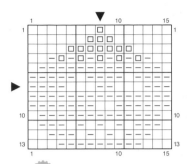

**16**
Stitch Count: 13 x 12
Cross-stitch

☐ B5200
☐ 369
— 310

Straight Stitch ▶

↳ 666

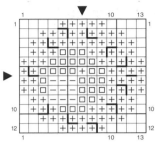

**17**
Stitch Count: 9 x 16
Cross-stitch  ☐ 369

Straight Stitch  ↳ 369

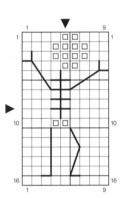

**18**
Stitch Count: 11 x 12
Cross-stitch  ☐ 369

Straight Stitch  ↳ 369

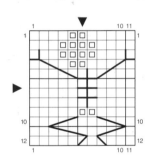

**19**
Stitch Count: 15 x 6
Cross-stitch  ☐ 369

Straight Stitch  ↳ 369

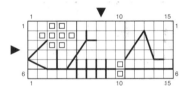

**20**
Stitch Count: 7 x 6
Cross-stitch  ☐ 369

Straight Stitch  ↳ 369

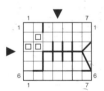

**21**
Stitch Count: 25 x 21
Cross-stitch

☐ B5200
☐ 434

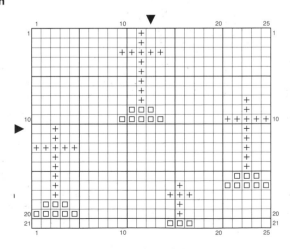

# Spaced Out (from page 14)

**Fabric:** Aida 14 count/ 310 (black)
**Thread:** DMC No. 25 floss
**Stitch Density:** 2 strands

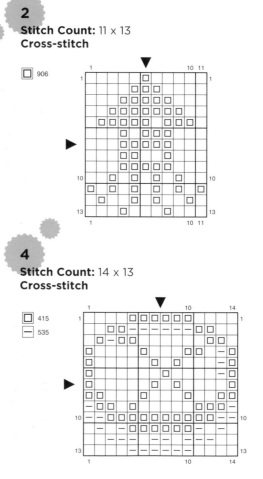

**1**
**Stitch Count:** 13 x 8
**Cross-stitch**

| | |
|---|---|
| ☐ | 157 |
| — | 415 |
| ✕ | 972 |
| ✳ | 798 |

**2**
**Stitch Count:** 11 x 13
**Cross-stitch**

| | |
|---|---|
| ☐ | 906 |

**3**
**Stitch Count:** 11 x 13
**Cross-stitch**

| | |
|---|---|
| ☐ | 893 |

**4**
**Stitch Count:** 14 x 13
**Cross-stitch**

| | |
|---|---|
| ☐ | 415 |
| — | 535 |

**5**

**Stitch Count:** 16 x 12
**Cross-stitch**

□ 415
— 535

**Straight Stitch** ⌐ 535

**6**

**Stitch Count:** 16 x 14
**Cross-stitch**

□ 415
— 535

**Straight Stitch** ⌐ 535
‥⋮ 972

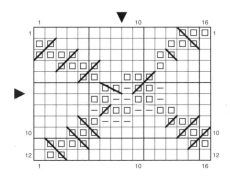

**7**

**Stitch Count:** 24 x 20
**Cross-stitch**

E B5200
□ 798
— 3790

**Straight Stitch** ⌐ 666

**Back Stitch** ⦙‥⦙ B5200

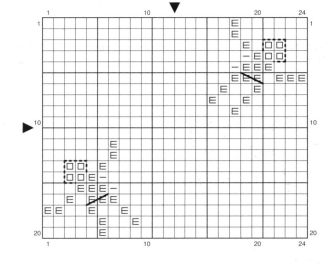

**8**

**Stitch Count:** 21 x 11
**Cross-stitch**

□ 436
— 972
✕ 801

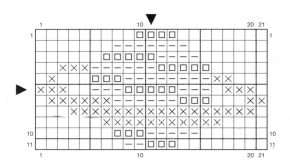

## 9

**Stitch Count:** 24 x 13
**Cross-stitch**

| E | 535 |
|---|---|
| ☐ | B5200 |

**Straight Stitch** ↳ 535

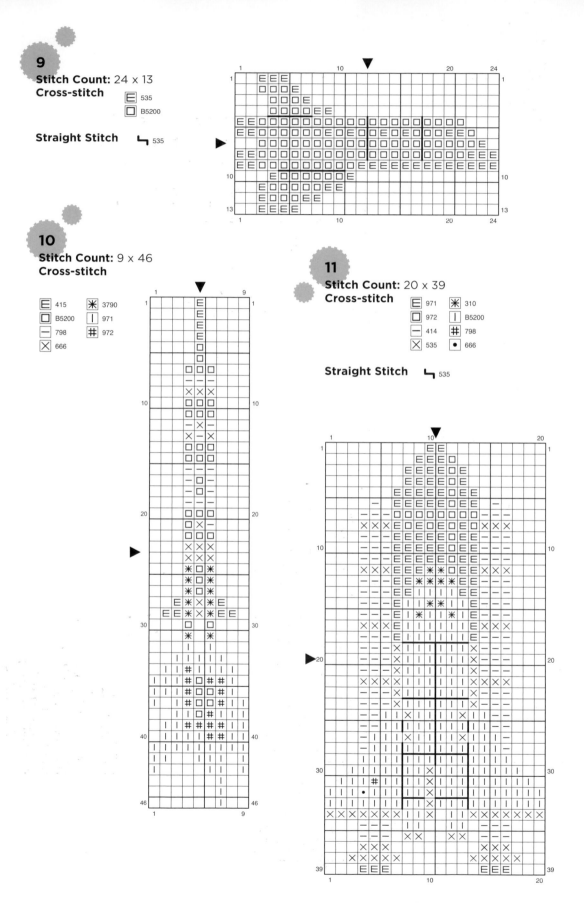

## 10

**Stitch Count:** 9 x 46
**Cross-stitch**

| E | 415 | ✳ | 3790 |
|---|---|---|---|
| ☐ | B5200 | I | 971 |
| — | 798 | # | 972 |
| ✕ | 666 | | |

## 11

**Stitch Count:** 20 x 39
**Cross-stitch**

| E | 971 | ✳ | 310 |
|---|---|---|---|
| ☐ | 972 | I | B5200 |
| — | 414 | # | 798 |
| ✕ | 535 | • | 666 |

**Straight Stitch** ↳ 535

**12**

**Stitch Count:**
**12a:** 24 x 4
**12 b:** 20 x 4
**12 c:** 15 x 5

**Back Stitch**

⌐ B5200

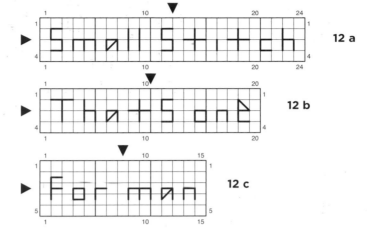

**12 a**

**12 b**

**12 c**

**13**

**Stitch Count:** 26 x 34
**Cross-stitch**

| ← 157 | — 893 | ✳ 971 | ⧣ 798 | ∨ 3790 | ‖ 436 |
| □ B5200 | ✕ 535 | Ι 972 | • 906 | ∧ 801 | |

**14**

**Stitch Count:** 10 x 10
**Cross-stitch**

| ✚ B5200 |
| □ 798 |
| — 906 |
| ✕ 801 |

# Grasshopper and Friends
(from page 16)

**Fabric:** Aida 14 count/ 310 (black)
**Thread:** DMC No. 25 floss
**Stitch Density:** 2 strands

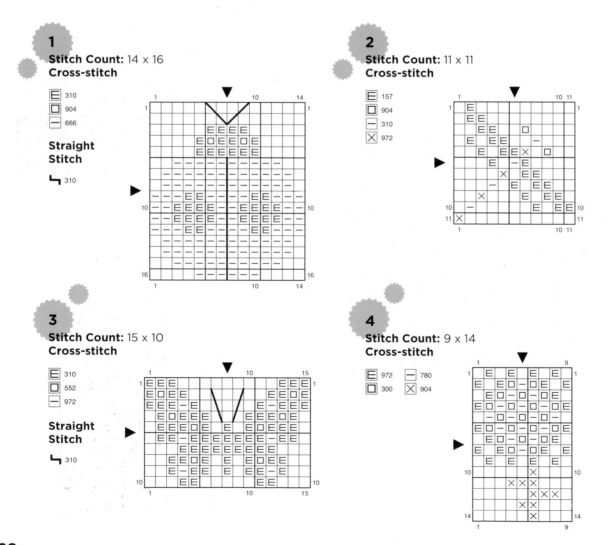

## 1
**Stitch Count:** 14 x 16
**Cross-stitch**

E 310
☐ 904
– 666

**Straight Stitch**

⌐ 310

## 2
**Stitch Count:** 11 x 11
**Cross-stitch**

E 157
☐ 904
– 310
✕ 972

## 3
**Stitch Count:** 15 x 10
**Cross-stitch**

E 310
☐ 552
– 972

**Straight Stitch**

⌐ 310

## 4
**Stitch Count:** 9 x 14
**Cross-stitch**

E 972    – 780
☐ 300    ✕ 904

**5**

**Stitch Count:** 11 x 20
**Cross-stitch**

| E | 310 | — | 666 | + | B5200 |
| ☐ | 798 | ✕ | 904 | | |

**6**

**Stitch Count:** 16 x 18
**Cross-stitch**

☐ 310
— 552
✕ 604
+ B5200

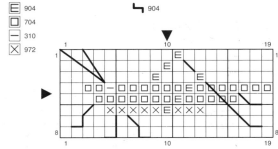

**7**

**Stitch Count:** 20 x 20
**Cross-stitch**

E 780
☐ 310

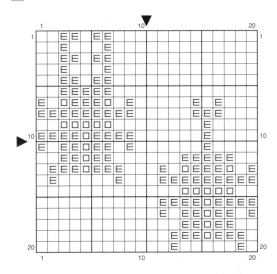

**8**

**Stitch Count:** 19 x 8
**Cross-stitch**

**Straight Stitch**

⌐ 904

E 904
☐ 704
— 310
✕ 972

**9**

**Stitch Count:** 15 x 18
**Cross-stitch**

| E | 780 | — | 666 | + | B5200 |
| ☐ | 904 | ✕ | 604 | | |

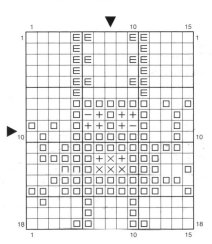

## 10

**Stitch Count:** 16 x 18
**Cross-stitch**

| E 300 | — 971 |
| 310 | + B5200 |

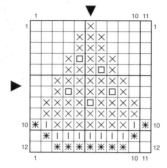

## 11

**Stitch Count:** 11 x 12
**Cross-stitch**

| 310 | ✳ 904 |
| ✕ 666 | | 745 |

## 12

**Stitch Count:** 15 x 18
**Cross-stitch**

| E 310 | — 666 |
| 798 | + B5200 |

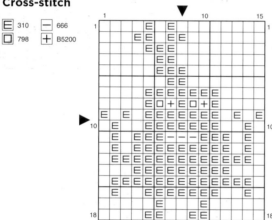

## 13

**Stitch Count:** 16 x 22
**Cross-stitch**

| E 971 |
| 798 |
| — 310 |
| + B5200 |

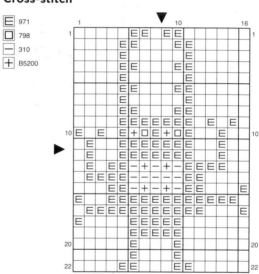

## 14

**Stitch Count:** 22 x 19
**Cross-stitch**

| E 904 |
| 745 |
| — 310 |
| ✕ 704 |

**Straight Stitch**

⌐ 904

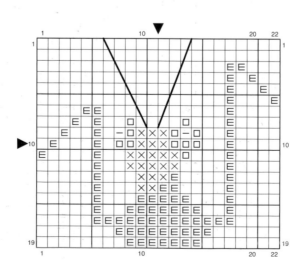

## 15

**Stitch Count:** 14 x 8
**Cross-stitch**

E  310
☐  666

**Straight
Stitch**

└  310

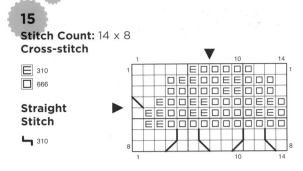

## 16

**Stitch Count:** 15 x 7
**Cross-stitch**

E  552
☐  310
—  745

**Straight
Stitch**

└  310

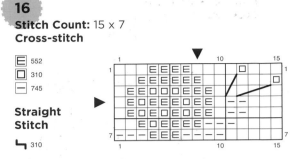

## 17

**Stitch Count:** 18 x 9
**Cross-stitch**

E  780
☐  310

**Back
Stitch**

┐  310

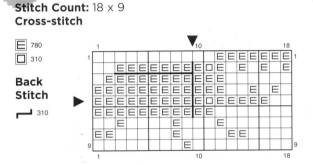

## 18

**Stitch Count:** 17 x 11
**Cross-stitch**

E  300
☐  310

**Straight
Stitch**

└  310

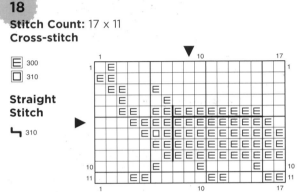

## 19

**Stitch Count:** 28 x 28
**Cross-stitch**  ⊞  535

**Straight Stitch**  └  310

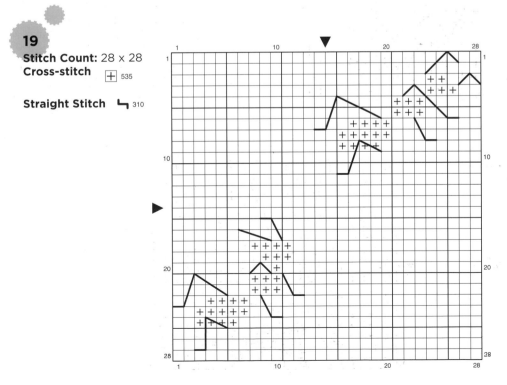

# Sea Creatures
## (from page 17)

**Fabric:** 14 count / Blanc (white)
**Thread:** DMC No. 25 floss
**Stitch Density:** 2 strands

## 1

**Stitch Count:** 27 x 16
**Cross-stitch**

| | |
|---|---|
| + | 310 |
| E | 798 |
| □ | 972 |
| − | 157 |
| X | 666 |
| ✻ | 415 |

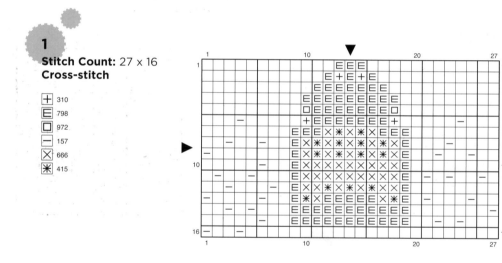

## 2

**Stitch Count:** 22 x 8
**Cross-stitch**

| | |
|---|---|
| + | 310 |
| E | 415 |
| □ | 972 |

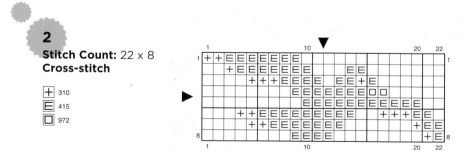

**3**
**Stitch Count:** 10 x 25
**Cross-stitch**

+ 310
E 666
□ 740

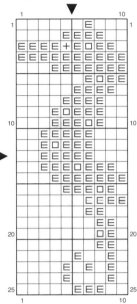

**4**
**Stitch Count:** 16 x 16
**Cross-stitch**   + 666   ○ B5200

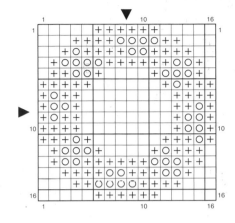

**5**
**Stitch Count:** 15 x 13
**Cross-stitch**

+ 310
E 666

**Straight Stitch**

↳ 310

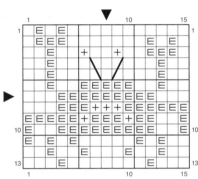

**6**
**Stitch Count:** 15 x 15
**Cross-stitch**   E 972

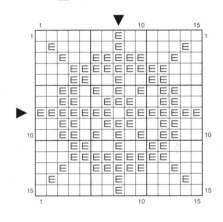

**7**
**Stitch Count:** 15 x 16
**Cross-stitch**   E 798

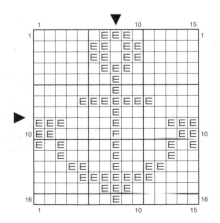

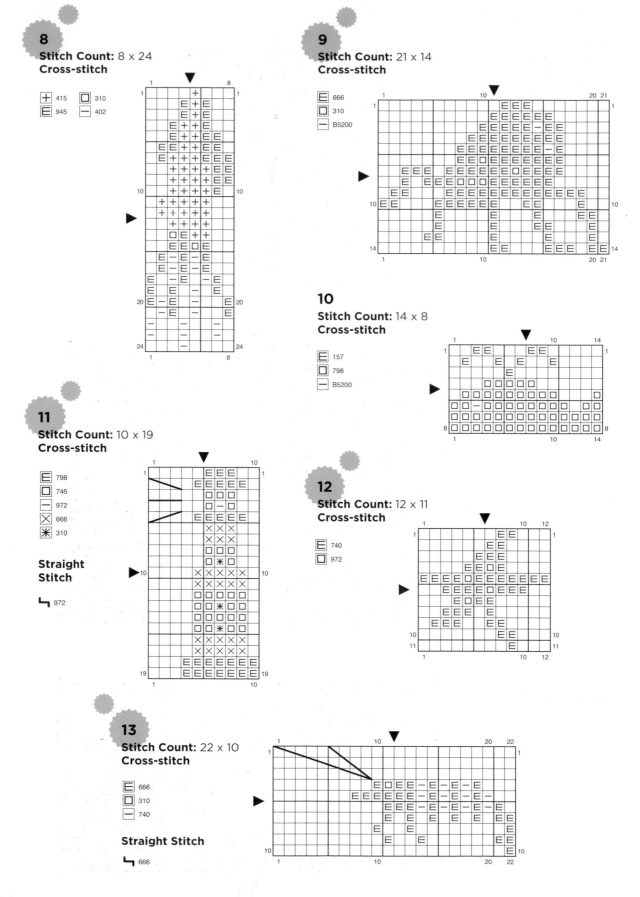

**8**
**Stitch Count:** 8 x 24
**Cross-stitch**

+ 415    □ 310
E 945    − 402

**9**
**Stitch Count:** 21 x 14
**Cross-stitch**

E 666
□ 310
− B5200

**10**
**Stitch Count:** 14 x 8
**Cross-stitch**

E 157
□ 798
− B5200

**11**
**Stitch Count:** 10 x 19
**Cross-stitch**

E 798
□ 745
− 972
X 666
✳ 310

**Straight Stitch**

⌐ 972

**12**
**Stitch Count:** 12 x 11
**Cross-stitch**

E 740
□ 972

**13**
**Stitch Count:** 22 x 10
**Cross-stitch**

E 666
□ 310
− 740

**Straight Stitch**

⌐ 666

## 14

**Stitch Count:** 19 x 21
**Cross-stitch**

| ⊠ 157 | — 666 | ☐ 972 |
| ⊞ 415 | E 798 | |

**Back Stitch** ⌐ 310

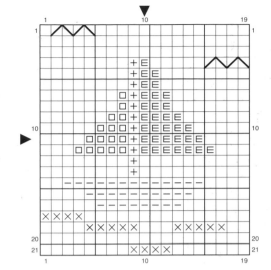

## 15

**Stitch Count:** 34 x 25
**Cross-stitch**

| E 702 | — 436 | ✳ 310 |
| ☐ 973 | ⊠ 798 | I 415 |

**Back Stitch** ⌐ 310

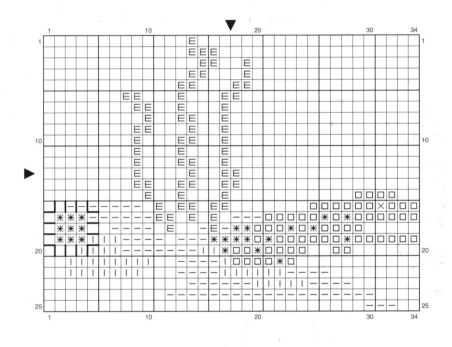

## 16

**Stitch Count:** 35 x 17
**Cross-stitch**

| E 740 | ☐ 798 |
| — 310 | ⊠ 973 |

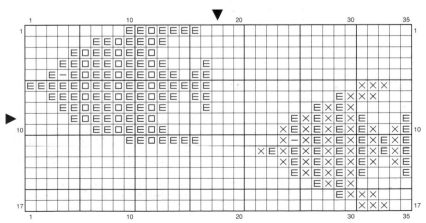

# Globe Trotting (from pages 18-19)

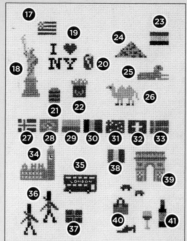

**Fabric:** 14 count / Blanc (white)
**Thread:** DMC No. 25 floss
**Stitch Density:** 2 strands

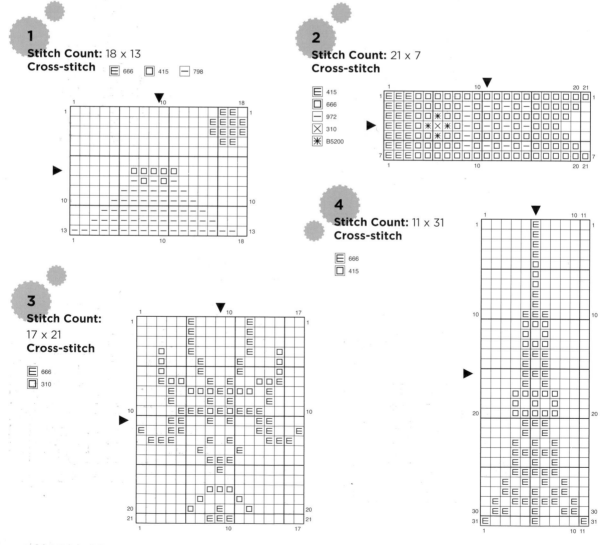

**1**
**Stitch Count:** 18 x 13
**Cross-stitch**

E 666   □ 415   — 798

**2**
**Stitch Count:** 21 x 7
**Cross-stitch**

E 415
□ 666
— 972
X 310
✳ B5200

**4**
**Stitch Count:** 11 x 31
**Cross-stitch**

E 666
□ 415

**3**
**Stitch Count:**
17 x 21
**Cross-stitch**

E 666
□ 310

## 5

**Stitch Count:** 13 x 15
**Cross-stitch**

E 310    □ 3856

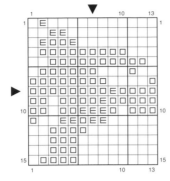

## 6

**Stitch Count:** 10 x 8
**Cross-stitch**

E 745
□ 666

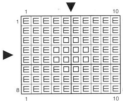

## 7

**Stitch Count:** 15 x 21
**Cross-stitch**

E 972
□ 310
— 745
X 798
✳ 414
│ 415

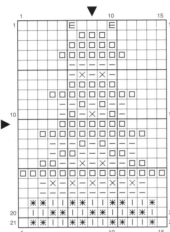

## 8

**Stitch Count:** 12 x 15
**Cross-stitch**

E 310

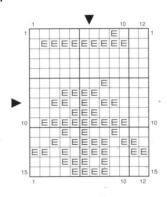

## 9

**Stitch Count:** 17 x 19
**Cross-stitch**    E 702

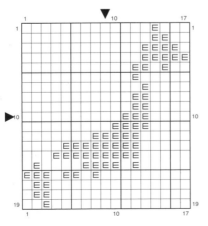

## 10

**Stitch Count:** 22 x 18
**Cross-stitch**

E 972
□ 801
— 666
X 310
✳ B5200

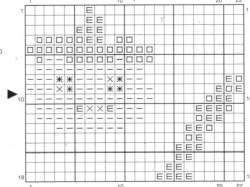

## 11
**Stitch Count:** 13 x 17
**Cross-stitch**

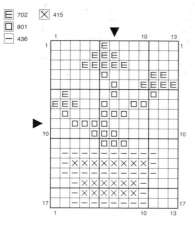

## 12
**Stitch Count:** 9 x 12
**Cross-stitch**

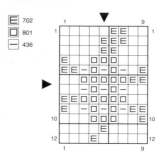

## 13
**Stitch Count:** 14 x 19
**Cross-stitch**

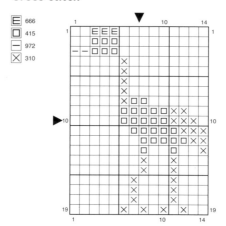

## 14
**Stitch Count:** 20 x 22
**Cross-stitch**

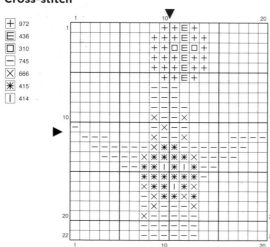

## 15
**Stitch Count:** 8 x 18
**Cross-stitch**

**Straight Stitch**
⌐ 310

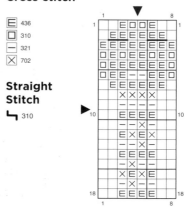

## 16

**Stitch Count:** 45 x 10
**Cross-stitch**

| | | | |
|---|---|---|---|
| E 666 | ✳ 3856 | | |
| ▢ 702 | I 972 | | |
| − 369 | # 310 | | |
| ✕ 321 | • 745 | | |

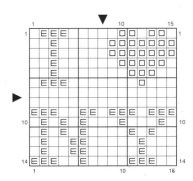

## 17

**Stitch Count:** 10 x 7
**Cross-stitch**

| | |
|---|---|
| E 798 | + B5200 |
| ▢ 666 | |

## 18

**Stitch Count:** 11 x 34
**Cross-stitch**

| | |
|---|---|
| E 972 | |
| ▢ 3817 | |
| − 3815 | |
| ✕ 841 | |
| ✳ 414 | |

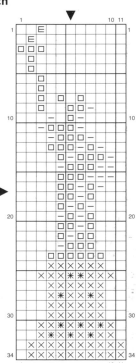

## 19

**Stitch Count:** 15 x 14
**Cross-stitch**

| | |
|---|---|
| E 310 | |
| ▢ 666 | |

## 20
**Stitch Count:** 5 x 9
**Cross-stitch**

+ B5200   □ 310
E 415   — 666

## 21
**Stitch Count:** 6 x 8
**Cross-stitch**

※ 801
□ 976

**Straight Stitch**   ⌐ 666
·⸍ 972
▪┐ 702

## 22
**Stitch Count:** 9 x 10
**Cross-stitch**

E 436   — 666
□ 976   X 972

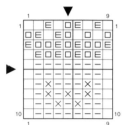

## 23
**Stitch Count:** 10 x 7
**Cross-stitch**

E 666   — 972
□ 415   X 310

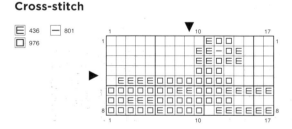

## 24
**Stitch Count:** 17 x 9
**Cross-stitch**

E 436
□ 801

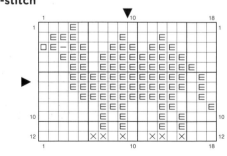

## 25
**Stitch Count:** 17 x 8
**Cross-stitch**

E 436   — 801
□ 976

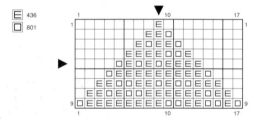

## 26
**Stitch Count:** 18 x12
**Cross-stitch**

E 972
□ 436
— 310
X 801

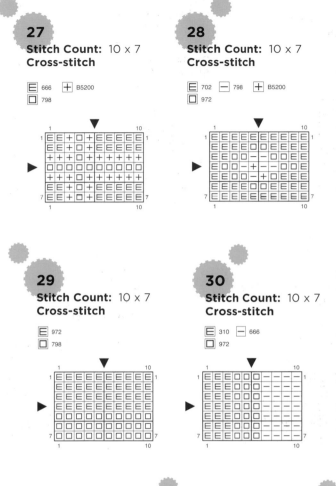

## 27
**Stitch Count:** 10 x 7
**Cross-stitch**

E 666    + B5200
□ 798

## 28
**Stitch Count:** 10 x 7
**Cross-stitch**

E 702    — 798    + B5200
□ 972

## 29
**Stitch Count:** 10 x 7
**Cross-stitch**

E 972
□ 798

## 30
**Stitch Count:** 10 x 7
**Cross-stitch**

E 310    — 666
□ 972

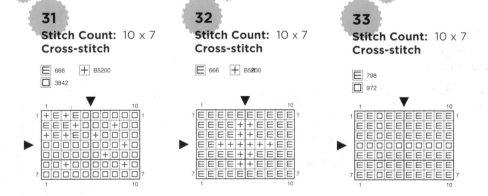

## 31
**Stitch Count:** 10 x 7
**Cross-stitch**

E 666    + B5200
□ 3842

## 32
**Stitch Count:** 10 x 7
**Cross-stitch**

E 666    + B5200
□

## 33
**Stitch Count:** 10 x 7
**Cross-stitch**

E 798
□ 972

## 34

**Stitch Count:** 19 x 21
**Cross-stitch**

**Back Stitch**

| | | | | |
|---|---|---|---|---|
| + B5200 | X 414 | ☐ 841 | ▪▫ 310 |
| E 157 | — 436 | | ⌐ 436 |

## 35

**Stitch Count:** 18 x10
**Cross-stitch**

| + B520 |
|---|
| E 666 |
| ☐ 972 |
| — 310 |

**Straight Stitch**

⌐ B5200

## 36

**Stitch Count:** 21 x 24
**Cross-stitch**

| E 310 | ☐ 801 | ✳ 972 |
|---|---|---|
| X 666 | I 841 | — 976 |

## 37

**Stitch Count:** 9 x 7
**Cross-stitch**

| E 666 |
|---|
| ☐ 3842 |

**Straight Stitch**

⌐ B5200

## 38

**Stitch Count:** 9 x 7
**Cross-stitch**

| E 798 |
|---|
| ☐ 415 |
| — 666 |

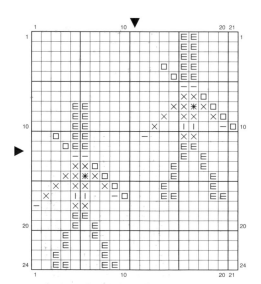

## 39

**Stitch Count:** 25 x 24
**Cross-stitch**

| | | | |
|---|---|---|---|
| E 414 | — 415 | ✳ 310 | + B5200 |
| □ 841 | ✕ 666 | | 798 | |

## 40

**Stitch Count:** 12 x 19
**Cross-stitch**

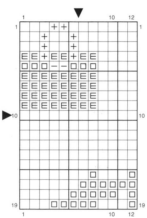

| |
|---|
| + 801 |
| E 971 |
| □ 666 |
| — 972 |

## 41

**Stitch Count:** 13 x 16
**Cross-stitch**

| | |
|---|---|
| E 552 | ✕ 436 |
| □ 310 | ✳ 414 |
| — 157 | |

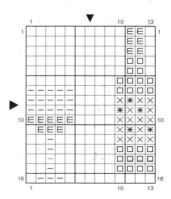

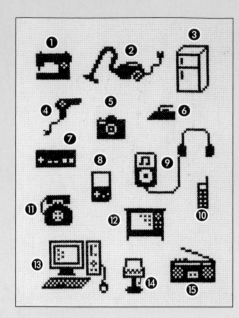

# Electronic Gear

**(from page 20)**

**Fabric:** 14 count / Blanc (white)
**Thread:** DMC No. 25 floss
**Stitch Density:** 2 strands

**PATTERN FYI:**
**Electronic Gear patterns all use cross-stitch with DMC 310 (black thread) unless otherwise noted.**

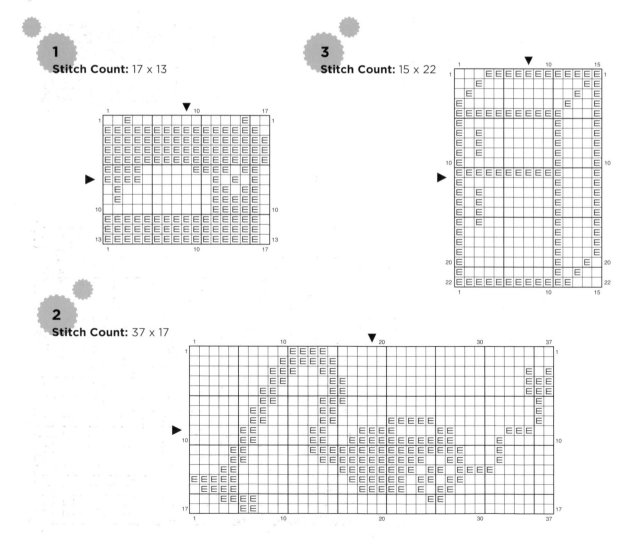

## 1
**Stitch Count:** 17 x 13

## 3
**Stitch Count:** 15 x 22

## 2
**Stitch Count:** 37 x 17

**4**

**Stitch Count:** 18 x 18

**Back Stitch used for detail**

⌐ 310

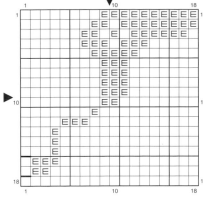

**5**

**Stitch Count:** 13 x 11

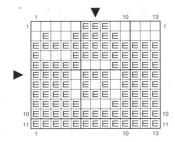

**6**

**Stitch Count:** 13 x 7

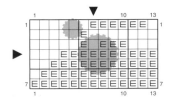

**7**

**Stitch Count:** 19 x 8

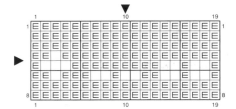

**8**

**Stitch Count:** 9 x 14

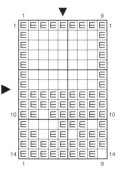

**9**

**Stitch Count:** 37 x 30

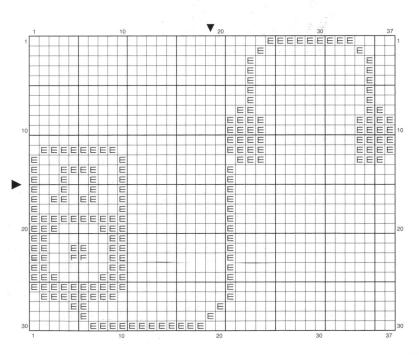

### 10
**Stitch Count:** 5 x 15

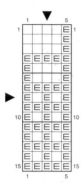

### 11
**Stitch Count:** 15 x 14

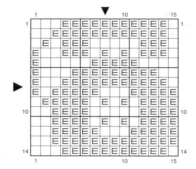

### 12
**Stitch Count:** 19 x 15

### 13
**Stitch Count:** 31 x 24

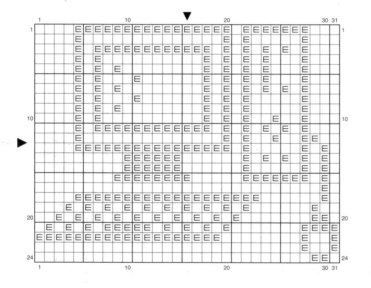

### 14
**Stitch Count:** 10 x 16

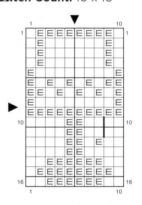

**Straight Stitch used for detail** ⌐ 310

### 15
**Stitch Count:** 21 x 16

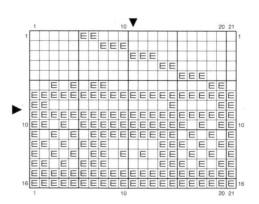

## Reading Pattern Charts for Projects in Part 2

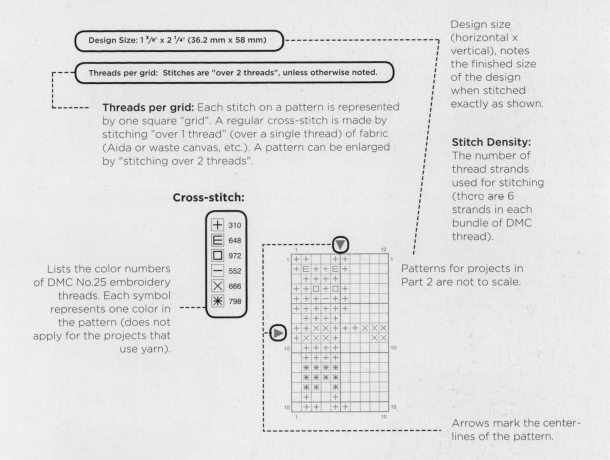

Design Size: 1 ³/₈" x 2 ¹/₄" (36.2 mm x 58 mm)

Threads per grid: Stitches are "over 2 threads", unless otherwise noted.

**Threads per grid:** Each stitch on a pattern is represented by one square "grid". A regular cross-stitch is made by stitching "over 1 thread" (over a single thread) of fabric (Aida or waste canvas, etc.). A pattern can be enlarged by "stitching over 2 threads".

Design size (horizontal x vertical), notes the finished size of the design when stitched exactly as shown.

**Stitch Density:** The number of thread strands used for stitching (there are 6 strands in each bundle of DMC thread).

### Cross-stitch:

| + | 310 |
| E | 648 |
| □ | 972 |
| — | 552 |
| ✕ | 666 |
| ✳ | 798 |

Lists the color numbers of DMC No.25 embroidery threads. Each symbol represents one color in the pattern (does not apply for the projects that use yarn).

Patterns for projects in Part 2 are not to scale.

Arrows mark the center-lines of the pattern.

### Before You Begin

Make the actual size pattern sheet before stitching to decide the layouts.

**1.** Make a copy of the pattern and cut it out.

**2.** Place it on the fabric or base you want to stitch on. Move it around to play with its placement. Consider balance and composition when planning the layout of a few motifs.

**3.** Cut the pattern paper larger when using waste canvas. Baste the pattern to the base fabric to keep it place before you start stitching.

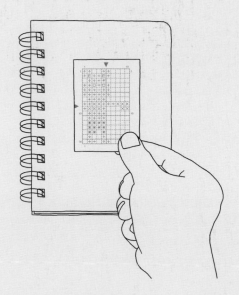

# CAPS (from pages 24-25)

**❶-a**
**❶-b**
**❷**
**❸**
**❹**
**❺**

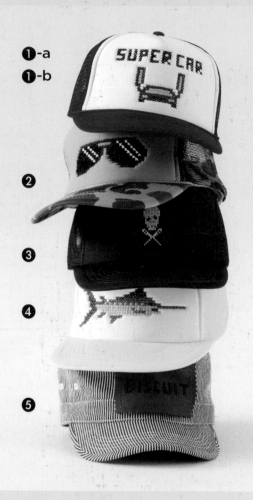

**❻**
**❼-a**
**❼-b**
**❽**
**❾**
**❿**

## Materials

- Blank cap
- Felt for patterns 3 and 8
- Thin suede fabric for pattern 5
- Stitch band, 1" wide (25 mm) for pattern 7
- Waste canvas, 14-count

**Thread:** DMC No. 25 floss
**Stitch Density and threads per grid:** Cap patterns use 6 strands
of thread and stitches are over 2 threads, unless otherwise noted.

## 1-a

**Design Size:** 4 5/8" x 3/4"
(116.1 mm x 18.1 mm)
**Stitch Count:** 32 x 5
**Cross-stitch**

E 310

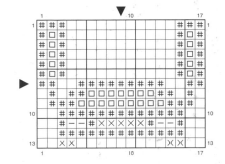

## 1-b

**Design Size:** 2 3/8" x 1 7/8" (61.6 mm x 47.1mm)
**Stitch Count:** 17 x 13
**Cross-stitch**

# 666  □ 996  — 972  X 310

## 2

**Design Size:** 4 3/8" x 1 3/4"
(112.4 mm x 43.5mm)
**Stitch Count:** 31 x 12
**Cross-stitch**

X 300  □ 310  —

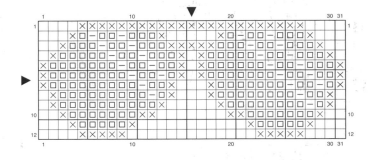

## 3

**Design Size:** 1 3/4" x 2 3/4" (45.3 mm x 70.7mm)
**Stitch density & threads per grid:**
Use 3 strands of thread over 1 thread
of waste canvas.
This design is stitched onto felt. When you
finish, attach it to the cap with fabric adhesive.
**Stitch Count:** 25 x 39
**Cross-stitch**

O 666
X 972
✳ 648

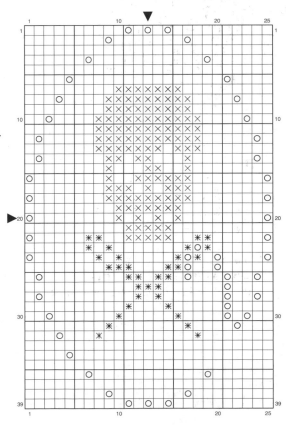

## 4

**Design Size:** 5 ⁷/₈" x 2 ¹/₄"
(148.7 mm x 58 mm)
**Stitch Count:** 41 x 16
**Cross-stitch**

| ○ | 930 |
| □ | 798 |
| — | 648 |
| # | 310 |
| ✳ | 157 |
| ❘ | 666 |

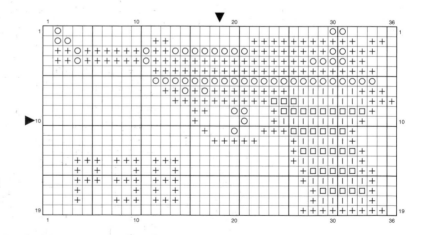

## 5

**Design Size:** 3" x ³/₄" (76.2 mm x 18.1 mm)
After cross-stitching on the thin suede, cut the edges
and attach to the cap with adhesive.
**Stitch Count:** 21 x 5
**Cross-stitch**

| + | 300 |

## 6

**Design Size:** 5 ¹/₈" x 2 ³/₄"
(130.6 mm x 68.9mm)
**Stitch Count:** 36 x 19
**Cross-stitch**

| + | 310 |
| ○ | 646 |
| ❘ | 300 |
| □ | 838 |

## 7-a

**Design Size:** 3" x ⁵/₈" (74.3 mm x 14.5 mm)

**Stitch Density & Threads Per Grid:** Use 3 strands of thread over 1 thread of waste canvas.

**Stitch Count:** 41 x 8

◯ 310　▢ 666

## 7-b

**Design Size:** 2" x 1¼" (50.8 mm x 32.6 mm)

This design is stitched onto 1" (25 mm) wide Aida fabric. When you finish attach it to the cap with fabric adhesive.

**Stitch Count:** 14 x 9

**Cross-stitch**

✳ 666　◯ 3078

⋀ 3827

## 8

**Design Size:** 3 ³/₈ x 2 ½" (87 mm x 63.5 mm)

This design is stitched onto felt. When you finish attach it to the cap with fabric adhesive.

**Stitch Density & Threads Per Grid:** For the letters, use 3 strands of thread over 1 thread of waste canvas and 6 strands over 1 thread for the rest of the pattern.

**Stitch Count:** 48 x 36

**Cross-stitch**

＋ 310
E 648
▢ 157
— 797
✕ 972
✳ 740
| 798

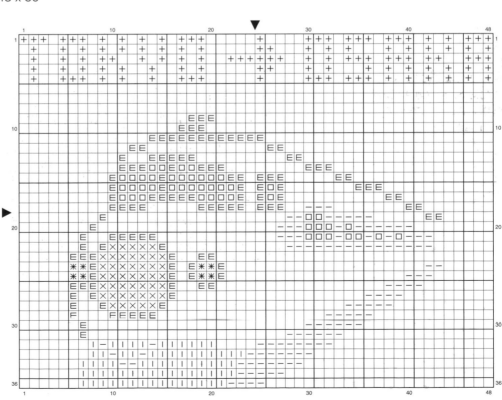

**9**

*The Japanese phrase "Yoroshiku" means "Nice to see/meet you." However, when it is written in Kanji (Chinese characters), as it is here on this cap, it's a reference to a famous Japanese biker gang from the 80's that put the phrase on their bike battle flags ... sort of like Godzilla saying "Nice to meet you!"*

**Design Size:** 6 ³/₄" x 1 ⁷/₈" (170.5 mm x 47.1mm)
**Stitch Count:** 47 x 13
**Cross-stitch** ☐ 552

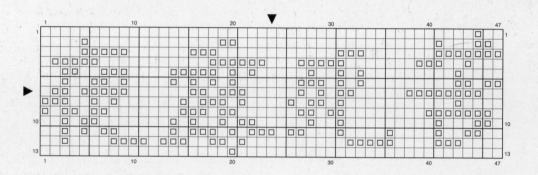

**10**

**Design Size:** 5 ¹/₄" x 1 ⁷/₈" (134.2 mm x 47.1 mm)
**Stitch Count:** 37 x13
**Cross-stitch**

☐ 310   | 666
# 702   + 972
✕ 3828  ✳ 996

# Time Travel Safari Shirt

**(from pages 26-27)**

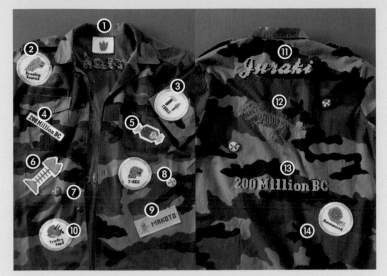

## MATERIALS

- Camouflage shirt
- Waste canvas, 14-count
- Aida, 14-count for patterns 2, 3, 8, 10 and 14
- Felt for patterns 5 and 6
- Scrap cotton fabric for pattern 7
- **Other items needed:** 3 covered buttons, safety pins, iron-on bias-tape (11 mm) and adhesive tape.

**Thread:** DMC No. 25 floss
**Stitch density & threads per grid:**
Patterns 1, 2, 3, 4, 7, 8, 10 and 14 use 3 strands of thread over 1 thread of fabric. Patterns 5, 6, 9, 11, 12 and 13 use 6 strands of thread over 2 threads of fabric.

## 1

**Design Size:** 1 ⅛" x 1 ⅜" (29 mm x 34 mm)
**Stitch Count:** 16 x 19
**Cross-stitch**

| + | 703 |
|---|-----|
| E | 972 |

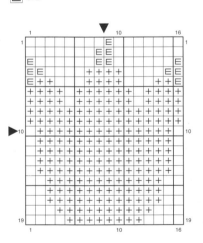

## 2

**Design Size:** 2 ¼ x 2 ½" (56.2mm x 65.3 mm)
**Stitch Count:** 31 x 36
**Cross-stitch**

| − | 972 | I | 666 | < | 894 |
|---|-----|---|-----|---|-----|
| X | 310 | # | 648 | U | 798 |

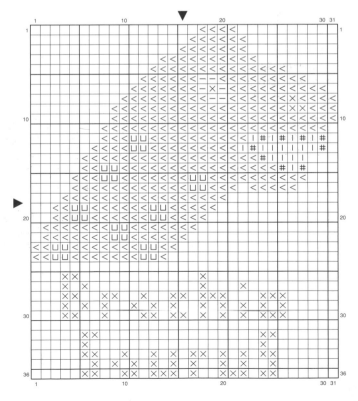

## 3

**Design Size:** 1 ⁷/₈" x 2" (47.1mm x 48.9 mm)
**Stitch Count:** 26 x 27
**Cross-stitch**

| ✕ 310 | ＃ 648 | Ⅴ 434 |
| Ⅰ 666 | ● 646 | |

## 4

**Design Size:** 5 ½" x ¾" (141.5 mm x 16.3 mm)
**Stitch Count:** 78 x 9
**Cross-stitch**  Ｅ 310

## 5

**Design Size:** 3 ½" x 1 ½" (90.7 mm x 36.2 mm)
**Stitch Count:** 25 x 10
**Cross-stitch**

| ● 300 | ✳ 740 |
| ＃ 434 | Ⅴ ECRU |
| Ⅰ 648 | |

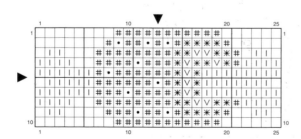

## 6

**Design Size:** 4 ³⁄₄" x 2 ¹⁄₈" (119.7 mm x 54.4 mm)
**Stitch Count:** 33 x 15
**Cross-stitch**

∧ 893
‖ 996

## 7

**Design Size:** ³⁄₄" x ³⁄₄" (19.9 mm x 18.1 mm)
**Stitch Count:** 11 x 10
**Cross-stitch**

+ 552

*Try this design in different colors!
I like DMC 972, 740 and B5200
which are shown on page 26-27.*

## 8

**Design Size:** 1 ³⁄₄" x 2"
(45.3 mm x 50.8 mm)
**Stitch Count:** 25 x 28
**Cross-stitch**

□ 702   ✳ 3818
— 972   Ⅰ 666
✕ 310   ♯ 648

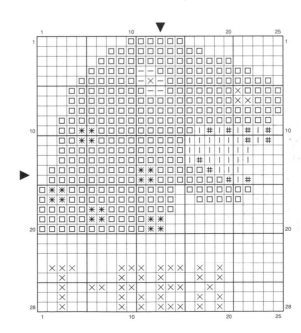

## 9

**Design Size:** 5 ½" x 1 ½" (137.8 mm x 39.9 mm)
**Stitch Count:** 38 x 11
**Cross-stitch**

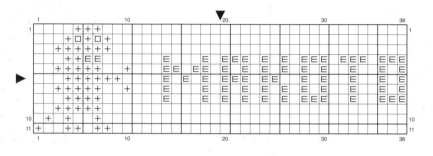

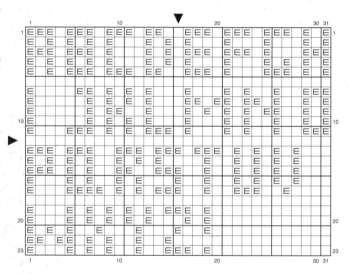

## 10

**Design Size:** 2" x 2 ½" (48.9 mm x 65.3 mm)
**Stitch Count:** 27 x 36
**Cross-stitch**

| | | | | | | | |
|---|---|---|---|---|---|---|---|
| ◯ | 740 | ✕ | 310 | V | 434 | Z | 437 |
| — | 972 | I | 666 | / | 720 | | |

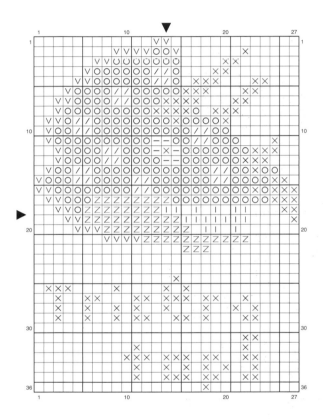

## 11

**Design Size:** 8 ¾" x 2 ½"
(221.3 mm x 65.3 mm)
**Stitch Count:** 61 x 18
**Cross-stitch**

| | | |
|---|---|---|
| Z | 310 | |
| ☐ | 972 | |

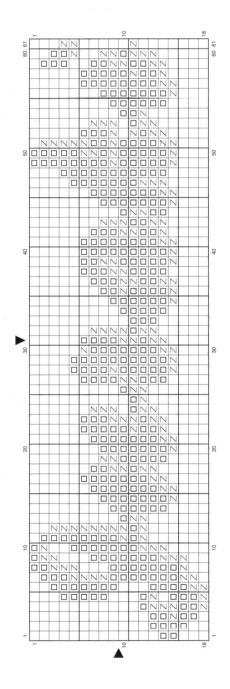

## 12

**Design Size:** 9 ½" x 6 ⅛" (239.4 mm x 156 mm)
**Stitch Count:** 66 x 43
**Cross-stitch**

⊥ 893

## 13

**Design Size:** 11 ¼" x 1 ¼" (286.6 mm x 32.6 mm)
**Stitch Count:** 79 x 9
**Cross-stitch** ☑ 310 ☐ 972

## 14

**Design Size:** 2 ⅜" x 2 ⅜" (59.8 mm x 58 mm)
**Stitch Count:** 33 x 32
**Cross-stitch**

— 972   ■ 666   ● 782   < 894
✗ 310   △ 434   ○ 799

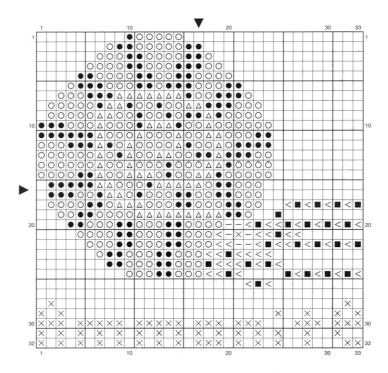

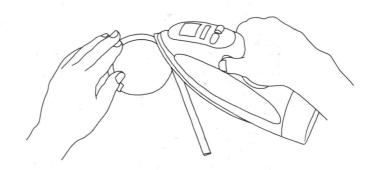

### Creating a Cross Stitch Patch
(Patterns 2, 3, 8, 10 and 14)

Once you've finished your cross-stitch design, trim the fabric close to the edges of the design, leaving a small border—the fabric piece will be about 4" (10 cm) in diameter. Use the 11 mm iron-on bias tape to create a border around the patch. Sew your patch onto your shirt. Looks good!

# 8-Bit Gingham Shirt

**(from page 28)**

## MATERIALS

......................................................................

- Gingham shirt
- Waste canvas, 14-count

**Thread:** DMC No. 25 floss
**Stitch density & threads per grid:**
Use 6 strands of thread over 1 thread
of waste canvas for all patterns.

---

### 1

**Design Size:** 1 ⅛" × ¾" (27.2 mm × 18.1 mm)
**Stitch Count:** 15 × 10
**Cross-stitch**

E E980

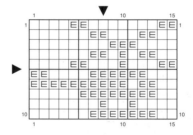

### 2

**Design Size:** 1 ⅝" × ⅝" (41.7 mm × 16.3 mm)
**Stitch Count:** 23 × 9
**Cross-stitch**

E E980

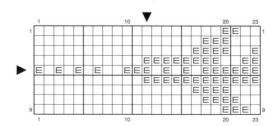

## 3

**Design Size:** 1 ⅛" × ¾" (27.2 mm × 18.1 mm)
**Stitch Count:** 15 × 10
**Cross-stitch**

E  E980

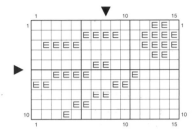

## 4

**Design Size:** 1 ¼" × ⅞" (32.6 mm × 21.7 mm)
**Stitch Count:** 18 × 12
**Cross-stitch**

E  E980

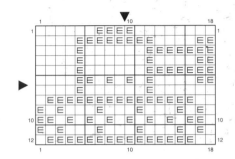

## 5

**Design Size:** 1 ½" × 1 ¼" (38.1 mm × 30.8 mm)
**Stitch Count:** 21 × 17
**Cross-stitch**

E  E980

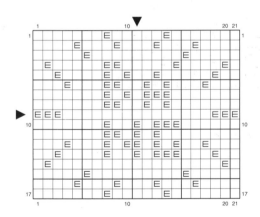

## 6

**Design Size:** 1 ⅛" × ¾" (27.2 mm × 18.1 mm)
**Stitch Count:** 15 × 10
**Cross-stitch**

E  E980

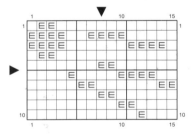

**7**

**Design Size:** 1 ¼" x ⅞" (32.6 mm x 21.7 mm)
**Stitch Count:** 18 x 12
**Cross-stitch**

E E980

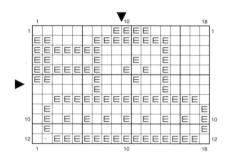

**8**

**Design Size:** 1 ⅜" x 1 ⅛" (36.2 mm x 27.2 mm)
**Stitch Count:** 20 x 15
**Cross-stitch**

E E980

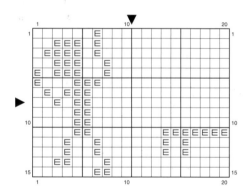

**9**

**Design Size:** 1 ½" x ⅝" (38.1 mm x 16.3 mm)
**Stitch Count:** 21 x 9
**Cross-stitch**

E E980

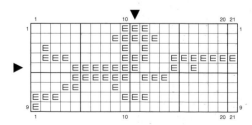

# Short Shorts

**(from page 29)**

## MATERIALS

- Boxer shorts
- Waste canvas, 14-count

**Thread:** DMC No. 25 floss
**Stitch density & threads per grid:**
Use 6 strands of thread over 2 threads
of waste canvas for all patterns.

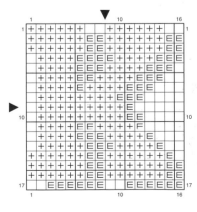

### 1

**Design Size:** 1 3/8" x 2 1/4" (36.2 mm x 58 mm)
**Stitch Count:** 10 x 16
**Cross-stitch**

| + | 310 |
| E | 648 |
| □ | 972 |
| − | 552 |
| × | 666 |
| ✳ | 798 |

### 2

**Design Size:** 1 1/8" x 2 1/4" (29 mm x 58 mm)
**Stitch Count:** 8 x 16
**Cross-stitch**

| + | 434 |
| E | 740 |
| □ | 310 |
| − | 666 |
| × | 798 |
| ✳ | 702 |

### 3

**Design Size:** 2 1/4" x 2 3/8" (58 mm x 61.6 mm)
**Stitch Count:** 16 x 17
**Cross-stitch**

| + | 972 |
| E | 310 |

### 4

**Design Size:** 1 3/4" x 2 3/8" (43.5 mm x 61.6 mm)
**Stitch Count:** 12 x 17
**Cross-stitch**

| + | 972 |
| E | 310 |

# Preppy Skull Sweater (from page 30-31)

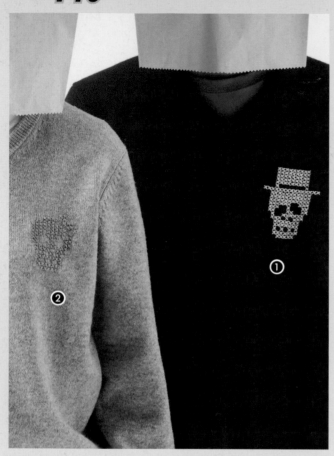

## MATERIALS
....................................................
- Sweater for each design
- Waste canvas, 14-count

**Thread:** DMC No. 25 floss
**Stitch density & threads per grid:**
Use 6 strands of thread over
2 threads of waste canvas for patterns.

### 1
**Design Size:** 1" x 1 3/8" (23.5 mm x 36.2 mm)
**Stitch Count:** 13 x 20
**Cross-stitch**

☐ ECRU

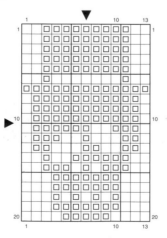

### 2
**Design Size:** 7/8" x 1 1/8" (21.7 mm x 29 mm)
**Stitch Count:** 12 x 16
**Cross-stitch**

○ 893

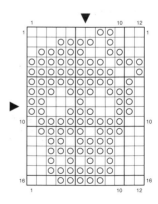

# Eco Bag for XS Lovers (from page 32-33)

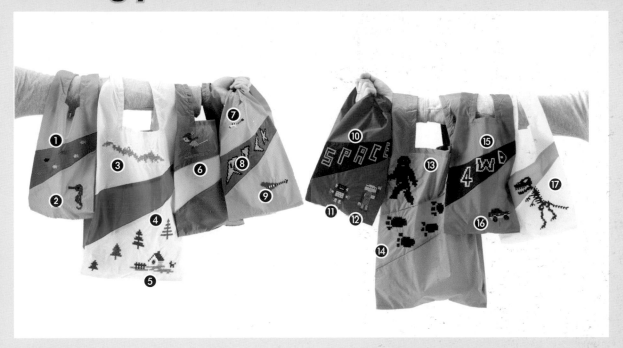

## MATERIALS

- Nylon bags
- Waste canvas, 14-count

**Thread:** DMC No. 25 floss
**Stitch density & threads per grid:** Use 3 strands of thread over 1 thread of waste canvas for all patterns.

### 1

**Design Size:** 3" x ¼" (74.3 mm x 5.4 mm)
**Stitch Count:** 41 x 3
**Cross-stitch**

| + | 310 | O | 972 | • | 552 |
|---|-----|---|-----|---|-----|
| ✳ | 798 | # | 907 | V | 648 |

## 2

**Design Size:** 1" x 1 ³/₄" (23.5 mm x 43.5 mm)
**Stitch Count:** 13 x 24
**Cross-stitch**

+ 310  □ 666  — 740

## 3

**Design Size:** 3 ³/₄" x ³/₄" (96.1 mm x 18.1 mm)
**Stitch Count:** 53 x 10
**Cross-stitch**  ○ 799  ⊔ B5200

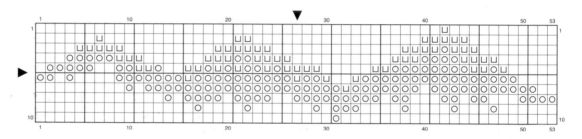

## 4

**Design Size:** 2 ³/₄" x ⁷/₈" (70.7 mm x 21.7 mm)
**Stitch Count:** 39 x 12
**Cross-stitch**

□ 937  + 3818

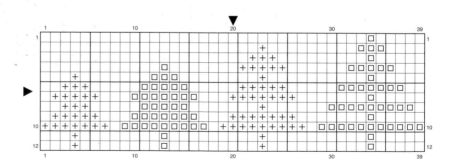

## 5

**Design Size:** 2 ½" x 1" (63.5 mm x 25.4 mm)
**Stitch Count:** 35 x 14
**Cross-stitch**

E 799  # 918
X 666  • 702
✳ 648  O B5200

## 6

**Design Size:** 1 ⅝" x 1 ¾" (41.7 mm x 43.5 mm)
**Stitch Count:** 23 x 24
**Cross-stitch**

+ 648  □ 3856  X 972  | 702
O 666  — 310  • 798

## 7

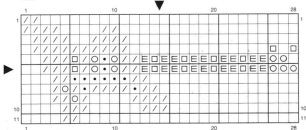

**Design Size:** 2" x ¾" (50.8 mm x 19.9 mm)
**Stitch Count:** 28 x 11
**Cross-stitch**

E 918  • B5200
□ 414  / 996
O 310

## 8

**Design Size:** 3 ½" x 1 ⅞" (90.7 mm x 47.1 mm)
**Stitch Count:** 50 x 26
**Cross-stitch**

○ 310
✳ 972

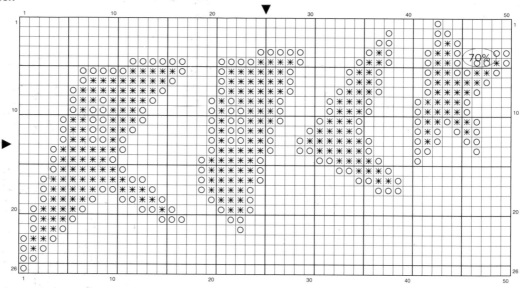

## 9

**Design Size:** 2" x ⅞"
(50.8 mm x 21.7 mm)
**Stitch Count:** 28 x 12
**Cross-stitch**

□ 414
# 310
• B5200
○ 552

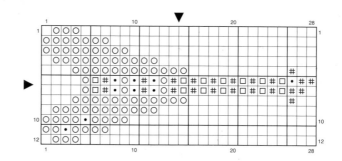

## 10

**Design Size:** 3" x 1 ⅛" (76.2 mm x 29 mm)
**Stitch Count:** 42 x 16
**Cross-stitch**

+ 702

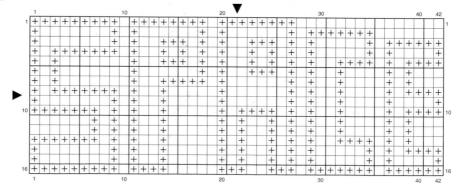

## 11

**Design Size:** 1 ³/₈" x 1 ¼" (36.2 mm x 32.6 mm)
**Stitch Count:** 20 x 18
**Cross-stitch**

| + | 702 |
|---|-----|
| O | 310 |
| # | 972 |
| — | 648 |
| X | 666 |
| I | 740 |

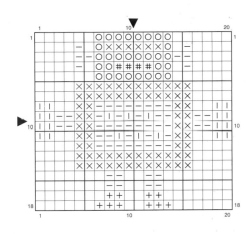

## 12

**Design Size:** 1 ¼" x 1 ⁷/₈" (30.8 mm x 47.1 mm)
**Stitch Count:** 17 x 26
**Cross-stitch**

| + | 702 |
|---|-----|
| □ | 972 |
| O | 648 |
| X | 666 |
| ✳ | 798 |
| I | 740 |

## 13

**Design Size:** 1 ³/₄" x 2" (43.5 mm x 48.9 mm)
**Stitch Count:** 24 x 27
**Cross-stitch**

| O | 310 |
|---|-----|

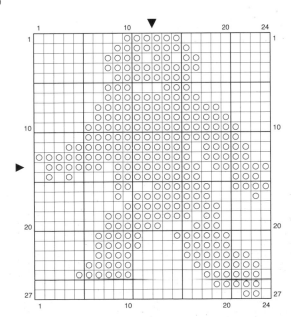

## 14

**Design Size:** 4 ¼" x 1 ⅜" (108.8 mm x 36.2 mm)
**Stitch Count:** 60 x 20
**Cross-stitch**

◯ 310

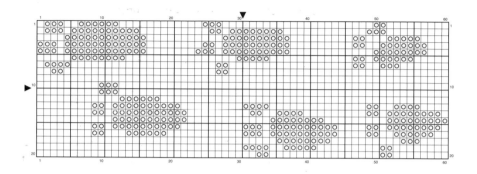

## 15

**Design Size:** 3" x 1 ¼" (78 mm x 32.6 mm)
**Stitch Count:** 43 x 18
**Cross-stitch**

+ 648

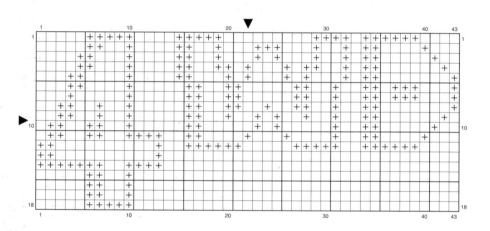

## 16

**Design Size:** 1 ⅝" x ⅞" (41.7 mm x 21.7 mm)
**Stitch Count:** 23 x 12
**Cross-stitch**

◯ 310
■ 666
— 972
✕ 648

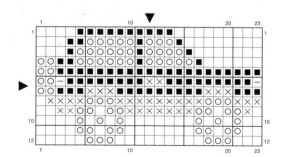

## 17

**Design Size:** 3 1/8" x 4" (79.8 mm x 90.7 mm)
**Stitch Count:** 44 x 50
**Cross-stitch**

+ 310

# Beautiful Bug Pillows (from page 34-35)

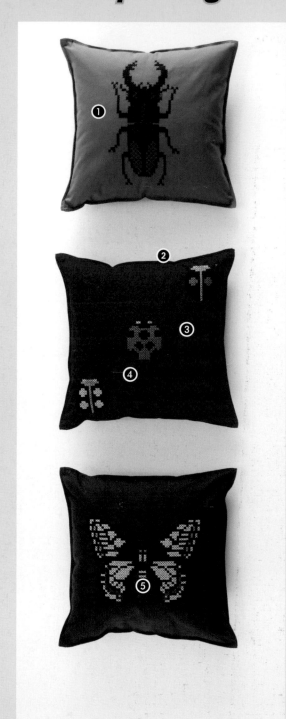

## MATERIALS

- Pillow cover, (solid color) about 18" x 18" (45 cm x 45 cm)
- Waste canvas, 14-count

**Thread:** DMC No. 25 floss
**Stitch density & threads per grid:**
Use 6 strands of thread over 3 threads of waste canvas for all patterns.

## 1

**Design Size:** 6 ⁷⁄₈" x 12 ¼" (174.1 mm x 310.2 mm)
**Stitch Count:** 32 x 57
**Cross-stitch**

| E | 720 |
| — | 801 |
| □ | 3371 |

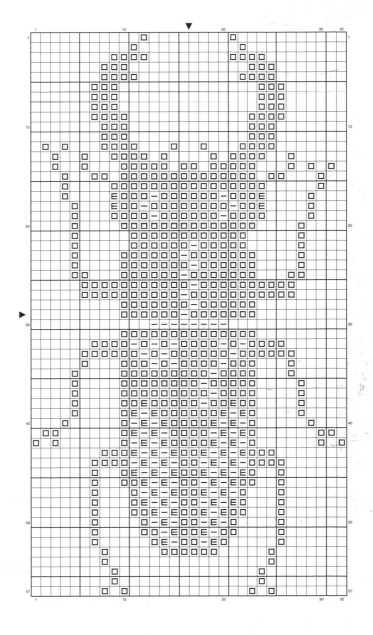

## 2

**Design Size:** 4 ½" x 4 ¾" (114.3 mm x 119.7 mm)
**Stitch Count:** 21 x 22
**Cross-stitch**

- ✚ 310
- E 972
- ☐ 646
- — 947

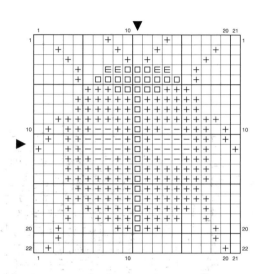

## 3

**Design Size:** 4 ½" x 4 ¾" (114.3 mm x 119.7 mm)
**Stitch Count:** 21 x 22
**Cross-stitch**

- ✚ 972
- ◯ 310
- ■ 947

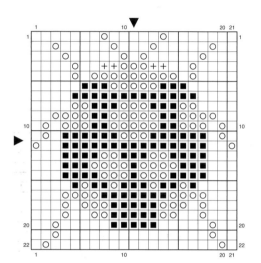

## 4

**Design Size:** 4 ½" x 4 ¾" (114.3 mm x 119.7 mm)
**Stitch Count:** 21 x 22
**Cross-stitch**

- ✚ 972
- ◯ 310
- • 646

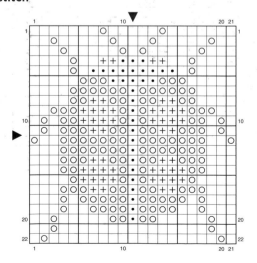

**5**

**Design Size:** 9" x 8 ³/₄" (228.4 mm x 223.1 mm)

**Stitch Count:** 53 x 41

**Cross-stitch**

- ⊞ 310
- ⊟ 972
- ☐ 840
- ⊟ 552
- ☒ 666

# Faux Tiger Doormat (from page36-37)

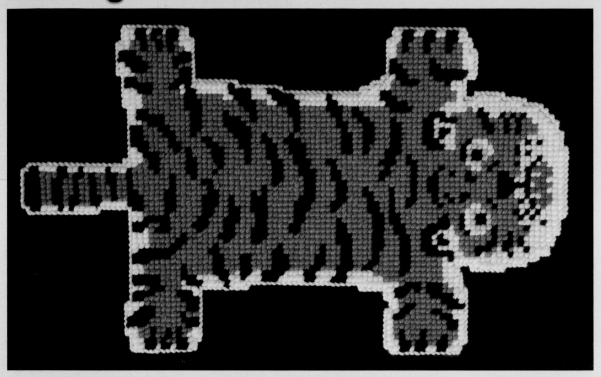

## MATERIALS

- Plastic canvas, (7-count),
  white 18" x 30" (46 cm x 76 cm)

**Thread:** Bulky craft yarn
**Stitch density & threads per grid:** Use 1-2 strands of yarn, depending on coverage, over 2 threads of canvas.

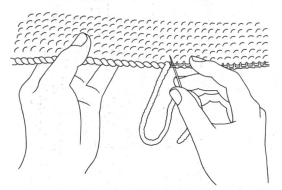

### Finishing the Doormat Edges

Once you've finished cross-stitching, trim the plastic grid close to the stitches. Secure the edge using an overcast stitch. Take the needle around and around the edge of the fabric, in the top of a grid, out the bottom, in the top of the next grid, out the bottom, and so on. It results in a very tight single ply stitch that will keep your tiger together!

**1**

**Design Size:** 18" x 29 ³/₄"
(455 mm x 755 mm)
**Stitch Count:** 60 x 100
**Cross-stitch**

| | |
|---|---|
| + | Black yarn |
| O | Orange yarn |
| I | White yarn |
| > | Yellow yarn |
| < | Pink yarn |

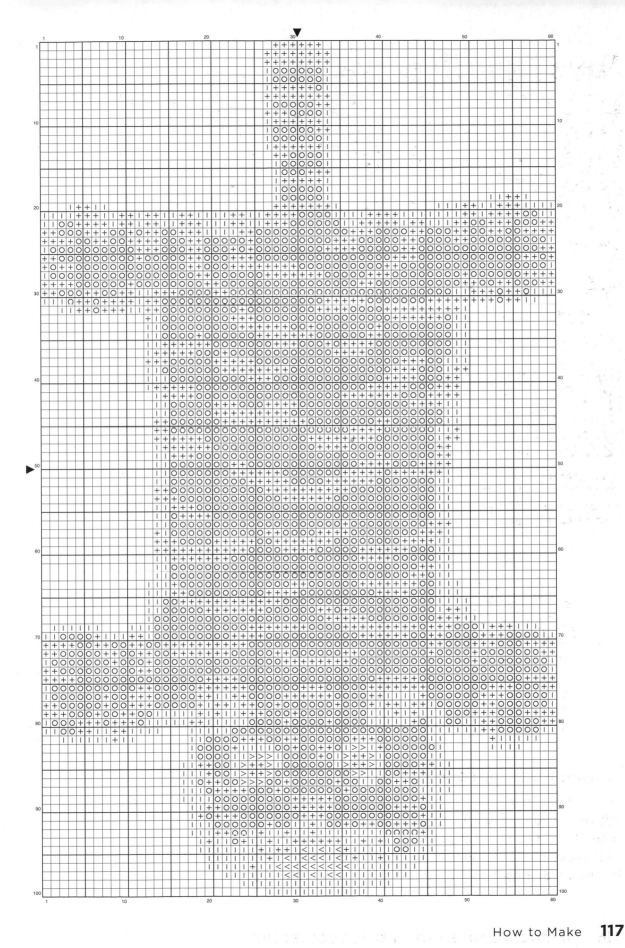

# In the Bag (from page 38-39)

## Materials

- Meshed pouch for patterns 1-5
- Cotton fabric, 1" x 1" (25 x 25 mm) for patterns 6-12
- Stitch band fabric, 1" (25 mm) width for pattern 13, and 2" (50 mm) width for pattern 14
- Key chain, plain silver (from craft supply store) for patterns 13 and 14
- Memo pads for patterns 15 and 16
- Lattice pattern vinyl pouch for pattern 17 and vinyl book cover for pattern 18
- Handkerchief for pattern 19
- Waste canvas, 14-count
- Covered button kit (from craft supply store) & elastic for projects 6, 7, 8, 9, 10, 11 and 12

**Thread:** Yarn for patterns 1-5; all other projects use DMC No. 25 embroidery floss
**Stitch Density:** 3 strands for all patterns using DMC thread, except where noted

## 1

**Design Size:** ¼" x 1 ⅛" (5.4 mm x 29 mm)
**Stitch Count:** 3 x 16
**Cross-stitch**

☐ Baby-blue yarn
— Dark-blue yarn

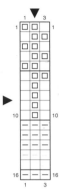

## 2

**Design Size:** ¾" x 1" (19.9 mm x 27.2 mm)
**Stitch Count:** 11 x 15
**Cross-stitch**

☒ Pink yarn
✳ Baby-blue yarn
Ⅰ White yarn

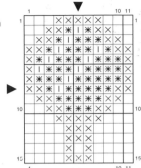

## 3

**Design Size:** ⅝" x 1" (16.3 mm x 25.4 mm)
**Stitch Count:** 9 x 14
**Cross-stitch**

☐ Gray yarn
✳ Baby-blue yarn
# Yellow yarn

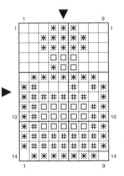

## 4

**Design Size:** ⅜" x 1" (9 mm x 25.4 mm)
**Stitch Count:** 5 x 14
**Cross-stitch**

# Yellow yarn
• Red yarn
∨ Purple yarn

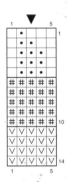

## 5

**Design Size:** 2 ¼" x ¼" (58 mm x 5.4 mm)
**Stitch Count:** 32 x 3
**Cross-stitch**

# Baby-blue yarn
∧ Dark-green yarn
‖ Brown yarn

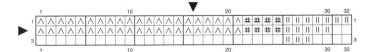

## 6

**Design Size:** 1/2" x 3/8" (12.7 mm x 9 mm)
**Stitch Count:** 7 x 5
**Cross-stitch**

 B5200

## 7

**Design Size:** 1" x 3/8" (25.4 mm x 9 mm)
**Stitch Count:** 14 x 5
**Cross-stitch**

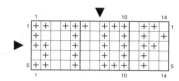 B5200

## 8

**Design Size:** 1" x 3/8" (25.4 mm x 9 mm)
**Stitch Count:** 14 x 13
**Cross-stitch**

X 310
□ 666

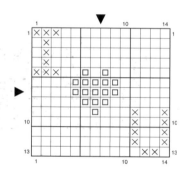

## 9

**Design Size:** 5/8" x 1/2" (16.3 mm x 14.5 mm)
**Stitch Count:** 9 x 8
**Cross-stitch**

| 666
• 3818

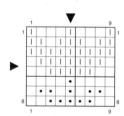

## 10

**Design Size:** 1" x 7/8" (23.5 mm x 21.7 mm)
**Stitch Count:** 13 x 12
**Cross-stitch**

X 310
| 666

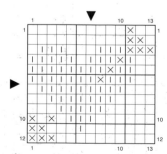

## 11

**Design Size:** $3/4" \times 3/4"$ (18.1 mm x 19.9 mm)
**Stitch Count:** 10 x 11
**Cross-stitch**

| V | 552 |

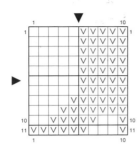

## 12

**Design Size:** $5/8" \times 7/8"$ (16.3 mm x 21.7 mm)
**Stitch Count:** 9 x 12
**Cross-stitch**

| □ | 648 |
| — | 894 |
| X | 310 |
| O | 745 |
| I | 666 |

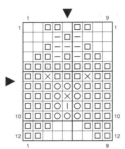

## 13

**Design Size:** $4 3/8" \times 1/2"$ (110.6 mm x 14.5 mm)
**Stitch Count:** 61 x 8
**Cross-stitch**   | X | 310

## 14

**Design Size:** $3 1/4" \times 1 1/2"$ (81.6 mm x 39.9 mm)
**Stitch Count:** 45 x 22
**Cross-stitch**

| □ | 602 |
| — | 310 |
| O | 666 |
| V | B5200 |

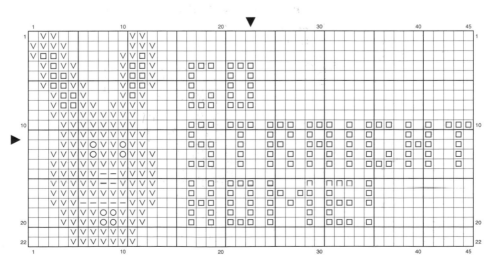

## 15

**Design Size:** 1 ¼" x 1 ⅜" (32.6 mm x 36.2 mm)
**Stitch Density & Threads Per Grid:** Use 6 strands of thread over 2 threads
**Stitch Count:** 9 x 10
**Cross-stitch**

- + 310
- □ 666
- ○ B5200

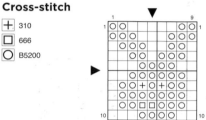

## 16

**Design Size:** 1 ¾" x 2 ⅛" (43.5 mm x 54.4 mm)
**Stitch Density & Threads Per Grid:** Use 6 strands of thread over 2 threads
**Stitch Count:** 12 x 15
**Cross-stitch**

- □ 996
- ✳ 666
- I 906
- # 718
- < 972
- Z 648

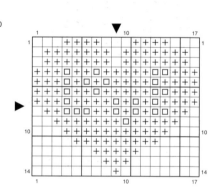

## 17

**Design Size:** 1 ½" x 2 ⅝" (39.9 mm x 67.1 mm)
**Stitch Count:** 22 x 37
**Cross-stitch**

- + 310
- E 677
- □ 676
- — 437
- X 840
- ✳ 976
- I 666
- E 677
- + 310

## 17-a

**Design Size:** 1 ¼" x 1" (30.8 mm x 25.4 mm)
**Stitch Count:** 17 x 14
**Cross-stitch**

- + 666
- □ B5200

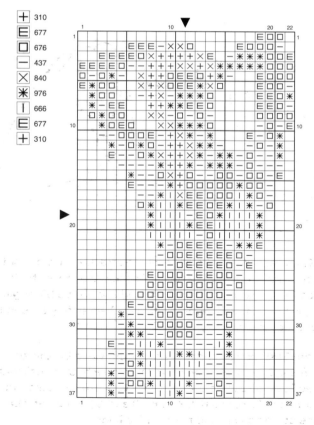

## 18

**Design Size:** 2 ⅛" x 5 ¼" (54.4 mm x 134.2 mm)
**Stitch density & threads per grid:** Use 6 strands of thread over 2 threads
**Stitch Count:** 15 x 37
**Cross-stitch**

☐ 798   ✗ 3031   | 436   || 611
— 413   ✳ 435   V 434   / 996

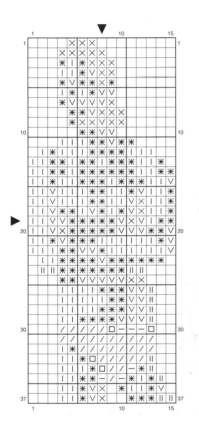

## 19

**Design Size:** 1 ⅛" x ½" (29 mm x 14.5 mm)
**Stitch Count:** 16 x 8
**Cross-stitch**

E 702   — 310
☐ 3818   ✗ 666

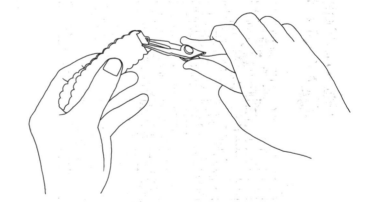

**Assemble the Key Chain:** You will need pliers to attach your cross-stitch design to the key chain (projects 13 and 14). Position the cross-stitch fabric in between the edges of the metal clip and add a little bit of glue. With the pliers, pinch the metal edges of the key chain tightly around the cross-stitch fabric. Let the glue dry.

**Make the Covered Button:** You can make a button with a button kit (available at craft supply stores). The kit will include a button shell with shank and back-plate that can be covered with your cross-stitched fabric. To make hair bands (projects 6,7, 8, 9, 10, 11 and 12) thread an elastic band through the button shank and finish with a knot.

# 3-D Panel (from page 40)

## MATERIALS

- Pegboards (3), 9 mm thick, 36" x 72" (920 mm x 1830 mm), pegboard holes are spaced 1" (25 mm) apart

**Thread:** Bulky craft yarn
**Stitch density & threads per grid:** Use 1 strand of yarn per pegboard hole.

**1**
**Design Size:** 108" x 72"
(920 mm x 1830 mm)
**Stitch Count:** 104 x 67
**Cross-stitch**

| | |
|---|---|
| ☐ | Black yarn |
| ⊟ | Baby Blue yarn |
| ☒ | Pink yarn |

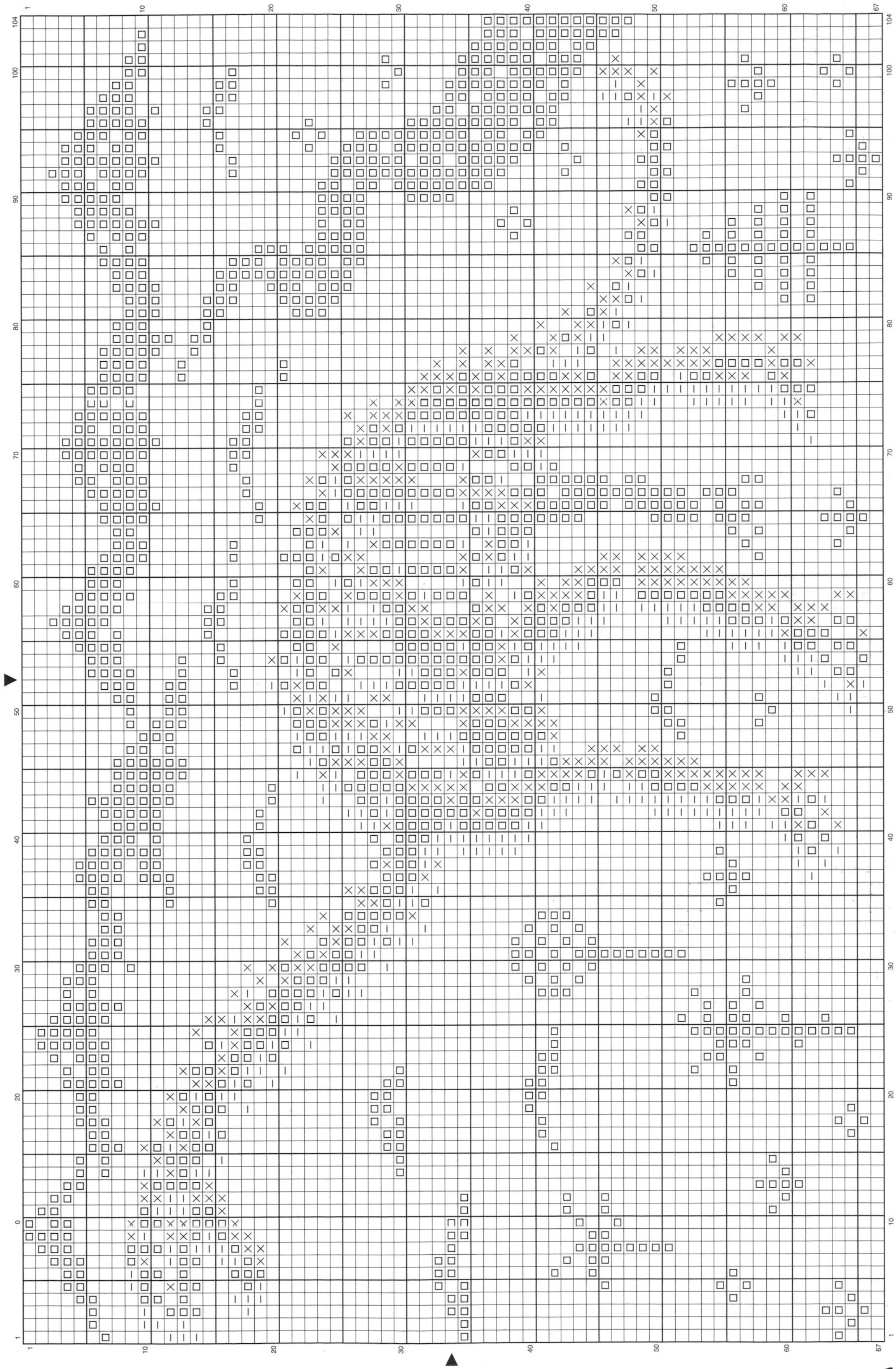

# THREAD CONVERSION CHART

Throughout the book DMC thread colors are noted.
Use this table to find equivalent Anchor thread colors.

| DMC | ANCHOR | DMC | ANCHOR | DMC | ANCHOR | DMC | ANCHOR |
|-----|--------|-----|--------|-----|--------|-----|--------|
| 301 | 1049 | 552 | 99 | 820 | 134 | 943 | 188 |
| 304 | 1006 | 604 | 55 | 825 | 162 | 971 | 316 |
| 310 | 403 | 702 | 226 | 829 | 906 | 972 | 298 |
| 318 | 399 | 646 | 8581 | 831 | 277 | 973 | 297 |
| 350 | 11 | 648 | 900 | 838 | 1088 | 3032 | 831 |
| 356 | 5975 | 666 | 46 | 839 | 1086 | 3345 | 268 |
| 413 | 236 | 740 | 316 | 840 | 1084 | 3346 | 267 |
| 414 | 235 | 741 | 304 | 869 | 944 | 3371 | 382 |
| 420 | 374 | 742 | 303 | 893 | 28 | 3781 | 904 |
| 433 | 358 | 743 | 302 | 898 | 360 | 3790 | 393 |
| 434 | 310 | 745 | 300 | 904 | 258 | 3815 | 877 |
| 435 | 1046 | 780 | 309 | 906 | 256 | 3817 | 875 |
| 436 | 1045 | 797 | 132 | 918 | 341 | 3828 | 373 |
| 437 | 362 | 798 | 131 | 920 | 1004 | 3842 | 164 |
| 535 | 401 | 801 | 359 | 930 | 840 | 3858 | 1007 |

# About the Author

After graduating from college, Makoto worked at a sewing and craft shop. Inspired by the amazing variety of materials to stitch, saw, drill and thread, a Gen-x-stitcher star was born!
To learn more about Makoto Oozu and his brave new world of cross-stitch, you can visit his website: www.theminthouse.com.

# Have fun x-stitching!